CHRISTIAN LIVES

The aim of this small collection of new biographies is to study outstanding Christians of the modern era, particularly some who have taken a lead in the ecumenical renewal of the Church in mission and unity. Thus a publishing venture may show some of the meaning of the words of Jesus: 'I have called you friends'.

A Man to be Reckoned With: The Story of Reinold von Thadden by Werner Hühne and *Zinzendorf the Ecumenical Pioneer* by A. J. Lewis have already been published. *Paul Courturier and Unity in Christ* by Geoffrey Curtis is in preparation.

AFRICAN SAINT
The Story of Apolo Kivebulaya

Apolo in 1930

ANNE LUCK

AFRICAN SAINT

*The Story of
Apolo Kivebulaya*

SCM PRESS LTD
BLOOMSBURY STREET LONDON

FIRST PUBLISHED 1963
© SCM PRESS LTD 1963
PRINTED IN GREAT BRITAIN BY
W. & J. MACKAY & CO LTD, CHATHAM

CONTENTS

Contents

ILLUSTRATIONS

Copyright: * Makerere College Library; † copyright Dr A. T. Schofield and
used by kind permission

MAPS

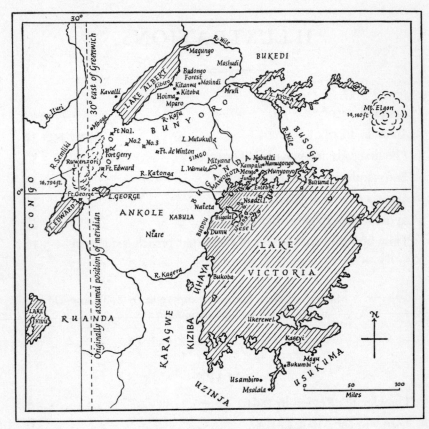

The Uganda Region in 1894

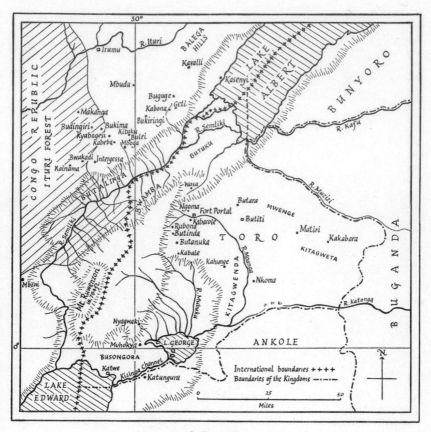

Toro and the Mboga Area

FOREWORD

by the Most Rev. Leslie Wilfrid Brown, D.D.

Archbishop of Uganda

Following St Paul, we say that the Church was founded upon the apostles and prophets. Christians throughout the world look back to the apostles of Christ with veneration and gratitude, yet they were not distinguished for scholarship or statesmanship. Judged by ordinary standards, the apostles had no particular achievements to their credit. All they did was to be faithful witnesses to their Master. They spoke and thought like any other men of their time, and the presuppositions of their thought and the forms which moulded their thinking were those of the Old Testament, the *Torah* of God, at once his law and his word to Israel. This was the really decisive and peculiar thing about the Jews, their formation by the Old Testament. The apostles of Jesus were working-class Jews and were probably quite untouched by European influences and the tradition of Greek thought which, in the form of mystical idealism, later penetrated and perverted much of the thinking of European Christians about God and man.

The abiding significance of the apostles lies in the fact that they were faithful witnesses to their Master and his resurrection and lived lives of obedience to the Holy Spirit. It is obvious from the New Testament that their obedience was not complete; they remained weak and fallible men; but they had no ambition and no plan other than to obey God, who spoke to them through the Holy Spirit and continually gave them fresh and deeper understanding of their Master and his message. As devout Jews they had always reverenced the sacred Scriptures; now they saw in them the promises of God to his people fulfilled in their Lord Jesus the Messiah. This conviction, that in Jesus the Scriptures were fulfilled, came into all their speaking. These very ordinary men became the pillars of the Church as it spread throughout the world. There was almost nothing distinctive about them except their complete committal to Jesus Christ, now known not in the flesh but in the spirit, and their understanding that for strength and wisdom they depended on God the Holy Spirit alone.

Apolo Kivebulaya was a man of apostolic quality. Although no other Christian can be equated with the apostles of Jesus who were witnesses of the resurrection of their Master, Apolo was in a true sense the apostle of Mboga Church and his life witnessed to the reality of the living Christ. It will be clear from the account in this book that Apolo had very little formal education. He accepted the Scriptures he was taught as the inspired Word of God, and his thought and life were wholly formed by that fact. It is related that he once visited the first class of ordination candidates to be taught in English. He glanced at the commentaries and other books they were using and then said, 'The Bible itself is the one thing you need. We must listen to God and not to man.' There is no trace in the records that after his conversion he was consciously influenced by an African world view or by the attitudes which his parents must have passed on to him. He was obsessed by the fact of Christ and of what Christ had done for him. He wished to be wholly committed to God and to be directed consciously by the Holy Spirit.

The results of Apolo's work were not spectacular. His importance does not depend on the work he did, or on the churches he built with his own hands, some of which are still standing, but in the proof he gave of the power of Christ to transform a man's life and to work through him.

Apolo was an apostolic man. The one desire of his life was to be faithful to his Master. Several times he had visions of Christ. He saw a man standing beside him as if he was his brother who told him to go and preach in the forest 'because I am with you'. Apolo confessed freely that he was frightened; he was scared of the cannibals and of other horrors of which he had heard, but it never occurred to him to disobey. His faithfulness was maintained by his life of prayer. In Africa it is the custom for the whole Christian household to gather early every morning to sing hymns and to pray together; that over, everyone will go to his work. Even many pastors seem to have no time of *private* meditation and prayer. Sometimes a European wonders if Africans are demonstrating that personal private devotion is not at all essential to the Christian life, but just a European way of doing things. But Apolo was accustomed to light his lamp from two till four every morning and spend the time in Bible study and prayer. He never allowed the difficulties and dangers of the forest or the long journeys in which he was constantly engaged to take him from this time of prayer, nor from the constant visiting of his people in their houses. One of his friends reports that Apolo used to worry very much that his teachers did not have the same vision and enthusiasm for the work as he had. He used constantly to call them together and teach them the importance of prayer and visiting.

Somewhere in his writings Baron von Hügel calls attention to the joy which characterized all the saints. This joy, stemming from complete confidence in the faithfulness of his Master, was noticed by everyone who has reported on his contacts with Apolo. We learn from his diary that he set out on 4 August 1919 from Mboga to attend the consecration of Namirembe Cathedral on 13 September, but he says nothing about the service, nor about the splendid brick building on the hill. One European who was present also remembers very few details of what happened on that day. She remembers only one thing clearly—the radiant joy on Apolo's face as he walked out of church in the procession of clergy. His whole life was marked not only by care for his churches but by a deep joy unaffected by the pains and hardship that he continually endured. Even in his last days of pain and weakness this joy was very evident. His most characteristic prayer seems to have been a kind of *Gloria* in which he praised God, Father, Son and Holy Spirit. In view of the paucity of his theological education it is most interesting to notice how his prayer and praise was continually addressed to God in

Trinity. This uneducated priest knew whom he had believed.

The third characteristic of Apolo was his courage, courage which came from his complete confidence in God's power to keep him. There is a whimsical touch about his story of meeting two lions when walking with a boy from Kabarole to a church in the bush. The boy suddenly noticed these two animals and, having never seen a lion before, said to Apolo, 'Sir, look at those cows'. Apolo merely replied, 'Yes, I've seen them', and they walked on their way.

Faithfulness, joy, and courage, these are three proofs of Apolo's abiding in Christ. And the greatest of all proofs is also evident; his people knew that he loved them. He did not despise the forest people as men of other tribes were apt to do; he slept in their little shelters and he ate their food. Bishop Willis described to me how he once went on a confirmation tour in the forest with Apolo. As they walked along the narrow tracks the news quickly spread that they were on their way and in every village they were welcomed by a great crowd of excited people. But they had not come to welcome the Bishop. Their faces were alight with joy as they called out, 'Apolo, Apolo', and rushed to embrace him.

Apolo Kivebulaya was God's gift to the Church of Uganda. He built the Church not so much by what he did as by what he was. The story of his life written in this book has few extraordinary or dramatic incidents to enliven it, but it recounts the steady attraction of Christ, glimpsed first on the face of a missionary and then exerting continually increasing power on a tough, uneducated young man until he was transformed and himself became in turn the instrument of Christ's love. The changed lives of the apostles were the most convincing witness in their day to the fact of Christ alive; the changed life of Apolo Kivebulaya and of countless others in the last eighty years in Uganda have been as convincing a witness to the same fact.

Apolo died in 1933, and the number of his friends grows less yearly. Written sources of his life-story and his teaching are scanty. Mrs Luck has done a great service to the Church of Uganda and to the world Church in her careful investigation and collection of memories of Apolo while these are still available.

PREFACE

The material for this biography is based principally upon Apolo's own diaries, which cover most of the years of his ministry. He was probably urged to write down the events of his life by the English missionaries. Although it is not clear when he first began to keep a more regular yearly record, his first diary contains accounts of the important events from the beginning of his ministry in Toro in 1895 until 1921. In another diary, 1922–9, he briefly tells of his childhood and early manhood. Five of these diaries are extant. They are mostly simple factual records and reveal little of Apolo himself, except for two or three sublime statements of his faith.

It is providential that these diaries have been preserved, as it is by this authentic material that other accounts of Apolo's life can be judged. Hitherto the three little books by the Rev. A. B. Lloyd have been regarded as authoritative. Unfortunately the serious discrepancies between his stories of Apolo and the authentic material render these works of doubtful value. These stories have, however, kept alive an interest in Apolo, and it was they which led me to undertake a more serious study of his life. I do not claim that the present work is without myth; legends and stories containing much truth grow around the memory of any outstanding personality, but the golden haze that surrounds Apolo must somehow be penetrated to see the real man. The truth about him, as far as can be discerned, is certainly remarkable.

A careful collection of all other material on Apolo has been made. The Rev. and Mrs P. B. Ridsdale collected the bulk of the stories and accounts from the people of Mboga in 1950. I visited both Toro and Mboga in 1957, and met many people who had known Apolo, including two old men who were among the first group to be baptized at Mboga in April 1897, and were themselves involved in the dramatic events under special scrutiny. The majority of these people were simple Christians, and I had the feeling that it would not have occurred to them to try and impress me with exaggerated tales; they simply told what they knew or believed, and all of them were delighted to talk about someone they had obviously loved. The consistent nature of all the material collected by me and others, from many sources, is in itself important evidence.

I have not attempted to make this into a contemporary type of study. I have simply tried to present the material in the context of its time. To those already well acquainted with the history of Uganda I offer an apology for once again covering this ground in Part I, but Apolo's later life cannot be fully understood or appreciated unless it is seen in contrast with the turbulent history in which he grew up and was involved as a young man. Part II deals with Apolo's ministry and includes an assembly of extracts from Apolo's diaries and accounts related by many different people. It suffers from a lack of unity, but as the value of this material lies in its spontaneity and simplicity I have refrained from attempts to polish or improve it.

Lest there should be confusion it may be noted that wherever the name 'Apolo' appears my reference is to Apolo Kivebulaya. The better-known Sir Apolo Kagwa, K.C.M.G., Katikiro of Buganda, is referred to throughout as 'Apolo Kagwa'.

ACKNOWLEDGEMENTS

My thanks go first to Mr H. B. Thomas, O.B.E., for his meticulous corrections to two drafts of the manuscript, and for his kindness and advice so generously given. I wish also to extend my special gratitude to the Archbishop of Uganda, Rwanda and Burundi, for much help and encouragement, also to Father Martin Jarrett-Kerr, C.R., and Bishop Sundkler of Bukoba for their advice. Also to Miss Glynne Evans, on the editorial staff of the Church Missionary Society in London, who steered me into the course that has led to the completion of this biography.

I am greatly indebted to the many people who have contributed information for this biography, and who are acknowledged in

Appendix C; but I would like to give special mention to Archdeacon and Mrs P. B. Ridsdale of the Ruwenzori diocese, who collected much of the material and translated some of the diaries, and my thanks are due to Mrs F. E. Ridsdale for writing out the translations so beautifully.

For hospitality and help during my travels I am grateful to Miss Kathleen Mawer, then headmistress of the Kybambe Girls' Junior Secondary School at Kabarole, Toro. Mr T. B. Bazarrabusa, M.B.E., gave generously of his time in taking me to visit all those who had known Apolo in Toro and for acting as interpreter. At Mboga I am grateful to the Rev. and Mrs Charles Rendle for their kind hospitality, and to Bezaleri Ndahura, who interpreted for me with painstaking care.

Very special thanks are due to Dr A. T. Schofield, who showed me his films of Apolo and generously gave me the plates of photographs taken by the Rev. A. B. Fisher in 1900, and his own beautiful photographs of Apolo. Thanks are due to Miss Ferrier, formerly librarian, and Miss Belcher, assistant in the archives department, at C.M.S. House, London, for their ready help, and to Mrs Joan Jetha and Mrs Marjorie Wallis for typing the manuscript.

Lastly I wish to express my affectionate gratitude to my husband and three children, who have suffered my preoccupation with Apolo with good-natured calmness.

Makerere, 1962   A.E.L.

Part One

HISTORICAL BACKGROUND

I

A BOY UNDER MUKABYA

'He who causes tears'

BUGANDA is, for Africa, an ancient kingdom. It is a beautiful and fertile land bordering the north-west shores of Lake Victoria. The endless flat-topped hills are clothed in dense elephant-grass and bush and are intersected by wide papyrus swamps fringed with dark forest.

When Apolo was a boy Buganda was a land of singular contrasts. The first European visitors to the country were impressed by the vigour of its people, and their government by a hierarchy of chiefs under the control of a Kabaka or king. Early travellers remarked on the handsome russet barkcloth dress of the Baganda, which distinguished them from their more naked neighbours, as did the neatness of their grass-built homes and the broad straight roads running from the capital out into the country. The extreme politeness of the Baganda was proverbial and they possessed a language rich in proverbs and folk tales. Real poverty did not exist, as the well-developed clan system took care of both old and young.

Yet beneath this attractive exterior there was a dark side to life in Buganda. The Kabaka, Mutesa I (reigned 1856–84), practised a despotism so cruel that it earned for him the name *Mukabya*—'he who causes tears to be shed'. Presiding at his capital in the heart of the land, he personified the tribal unity, and the submission of his subjects to his absolutism is expressed in the proverb: 'Kabaka Kimera named his house "Blacksmith's Forge".' This proverb meant that just as the blacksmith's shop has charcoal burning all the time, yet no ashes accumulate, so it is with the Kabaka, who always kills people, and yet they go to him.[1]

Mutesa I was a man of regal bearing, great intelligence and diplomatic skill, but as in the days of his predecessors, the killing of his subjects on the slightest pretext was the means by which he retained his power. His horde of executioners was always at hand to drag off and put to death or mutilate any who offended against his slightest whim, man or woman. Mass ritual executions were also ordered at times of crisis to propitiate the *balubale* or national gods, and thus prevent them bringing misfortune on the land.

All personal gain depended upon the favour of the Kabaka. The once hereditary chieftainships were now disposed of by his arbitrary will; promotion depended largely on military prowess and services to the Kabaka. As the desire for chiefly status was an overwhelming ambition of the Baganda, rivalry and intrigue made life at the capital precarious. The chiefs emulated the Kabaka with large establishments of women, slaves and retainers, lands and cattle, and they held cruel sway over lesser chiefs and their subordinates. Thus a chain of fear and subservience extended from the lowest peasant through all grades of hierarchy to the Kabaka.

The home of a pagan peasant

In the country far from the capital, life was less dangerous. Apolo's father was an ordinary peasant, probably holding land from the local chief in return for labour, tribute and allegiance in war.[2]

Apolo records briefly: 'I was born in Kiwanda on the way to Mutukula, in the district of Singo. . . . We were five children. Our mother, Nalongo Tezira Singabadda of the Ngabi clan, was a daughter of the line of princesses. Our father, Samweri Salongo Kisawuzi of the Katinvuma clan,[3] came from Bumbu in Busiro; he married our mother in the time of Suna.[4] As a child he had been a slave of the Banyoro; when he grew up he became courageous and speared many people in battle.'

Singo was one of the largest districts in Buganda, but because of its proximity to Bunyoro, which was the other dominant power in the Lake region, it was sparsely populated. Warfare between the two peoples was a yearly event; raids and counter raids added excitement to life, and were the means of procuring wealth in the form of women, slaves, and cattle. The principal chief of Singo, the *Mukwenda*, had his enclosures and country estates at Mityana, a place some forty miles from the Kabaka's capital. About twenty miles north lay the small lake Mutukula, one of the thirteen places of ritual slaughter in Buganda. Somewhere in this region Apolo was born. His father may have owed allegiance to the *Mukwenda* himself or to one of his sub-chiefs.

Most peasants lived in loose 'village' communities scattered about the lower slopes of the hills, with each family on its own plot of land or garden, perhaps only within calling distance of the neighbours. The dense growth of the cultivated banana trees almost hid the homesteads of conical grass-built huts. Most peasants had more than one wife, and each had her own hut. These were clustered around an open space or yard where the activities and festivities of family life took place. Life was leisurely. Basic needs could be supplied with a minimum of labour. The women and girls went out at dawn to cultivate and fetch water. When the dew was off the grass boys would herd out the goats. The midday meal was prepared by the women in cooking huts separate from the dwelling huts. In the afternoon women sat talking in the yard making baskets or mats or shelling peas. Men of the peasant class would clear new land, fell trees, and build huts; it was their task to make the barkcloth, to work for the chief or to follow him to war. In times of peace there was always plenty of leisure for sitting about, drinking beer, and paying calls; the favourite time for the beer drink was after the evening meal. This would be accompanied by drumming and singing.

In the banana gardens surrounding the homestead small spirit huts or shrines were built for the *mizimu* or spirits of the dead; here offerings of coffee berries, beer or occasionally a chicken were placed. Noonday was the time for the spirits to be abroad and the eddies of hot air that stirred up the dust and rattled the banana leaves were said to be the *mizimu*, which made the children run in terror to their huts. The supernatural was part of the structure of

Baganda society, personal wills were operative in all aspects of life. Besides the ancestral spirits, whose concern was with the family and clan, their world included a host of supernatural beings of national importance, collectively known as *balubale*; these were connected with natural objects like rocks, trees, rivers, and wild animals; also with legendary human beings noted for their skill and bravery; and the tribal prosperity and life force was believed to depend upon good relationships with them.

Fear was a dominant factor in life in those days. Man was never free from it, his life was hedged around with countless rules and taboos, infringement of them would bring swift retribution. All misfortunes and frustrations were attributed to evil wills, the malice of an enemy or revenge on the part of some unpropitiated spirit. People were at the mercy of the sorcerer, whose intermediary position between ordinary man and the spirit world gave him extraordinary powers; with his knowledge of poisons and human psychology he knew how to play upon their fears, casting spells or practising exorcism. He also was a very real source of fear in the community.[5]

Apolo's birth, which took place about 1864,[6] was noteworthy because he was one of twins, and among the Baganda the birth of twins was an occasion for great fear as well as rejoicing. This also meant that he would be singled out for the rest of his life. 'My name as one of the twins was Waswa.'[7] Special names were prescribed for twins, Waswa and Kato for two boys, Kato and Nakato for a boy and a girl, Nakato and Babirye for two girls. The parents also were given extra honorific names; the mother was called Nalongo (mother of twins) and the father Salongo (father of twins).

The birth of twins was regarded as an unmerited favour from the *lubale* Mukasa, the giver of children.[8] It was, however, an alarming gift, which necessitated the observance of complicated taboos and ritual in order not to offend the god and any failure would provoke his anger. This might result in the death of the twins or their parents or might even be extended to the whole clan. This frightening power was also connected with the twins themselves, whose spirits were feared should they die.

The death of a twin was a great calamity. It is mentioned that Apolo's twin died in early childhood, and Apolo himself records: 'If a twin dies the parents do not weep, because they fear the other twin may die also, or the father or the mother. They announce the death by saying the child has gone back and everyone knows what that means. The body of the dead child is put in an old cooking pot near the fire to dry out, as meat is dried.' When the appointed time is over they take the body away for burial and the cooking pot is placed upside down over the burial place; thus all who pass that way may know it is the grave of a twin and avoid it, lest the ghost should catch them. Women especially avoided the place and threw grass upon the grave to prevent the ghost from entering into them and being reborn.

Despite the unusual circumstances of his birth the child Waswa probably enjoyed the normal life of a small boy of those times. Children lived a very free life. There were many of them in the community and they spent their days herding the goats and sheep. Parents were indulgent and seldom checked or reproved a child, and by the time he was seven or eight years old he would be somewhat out of hand. Hence children of this age were often sent to the household of a relative; boys usually went to their paternal uncle, where they would be more strictly brought up. Parents were also eager to place a son in the household of a chief, where there were greater opportunities for advancement. A quick and attentive lad might be sent as an attendant to the Kabaka's court, with the possibility of rising to a chieftainship.

Apolo once told Bishop Kitching that as a child he had been employed by a witch-doctor to carry his paraphernalia. This witch-doctor was probably a *muganga*, a doctor who deals in antidotes and protection against spells. He may have been a relative, as it was not usual for people to place their children in the home of one who practised witchcraft. However, Apolo appeared to have learned something about the tricks of the trade, for he described the procedure adopted by his employer in dealing with sickness. 'He said that when called to a sick person the witch-doctor would demand his fee of a goat and inspect the patient, saying there was some spell

25

or charm set by an enemy. After dark when all was quiet he would go outside the house and bury a horn, usually a goat's horn filled with blood, carefully covering up his traces. The next morning he would proceed to smell out the charm; taking a bag of pebbles he would go in turn to every corner of the house, rattling the pebbles and listening to the supposed voice to tell him the whereabouts of the evil. Finally he would go outside and pretend to discover the horn which he denounced as the cause of the illness.'[9]

As a boy grew older he would accompany his father, or guardian or elder brother, on raiding expeditions, or perform tasks demanded by the chief, such as road clearing, building, carrying food or tribute to the capital, where also certain allotted tasks had to be performed for the Kabaka by the different chiefs and clans. The unwilling peasants formed part of the chief's labour force, and dreaded going to the capital because of the danger of being seized and put to death. All paths approaching the capital had to cross the swamps surrounding the royal hill. The slopes of the hill were covered with many grass huts, half hidden in the green of their banana gardens, and on the summit was the Kabaka's *lubiri* or royal enclosure. Here, surrounded by high reed fences with guarded gates, were courtyards containing the large grass-built audience hall, the royal dwelling houses, court houses, and shrines for fetishes. Outside these guarded fences were the fenced enclosures of the Kabaka's many hundred wives, attendants, bodyguards, and slaves, as well as the enclosures of all senior chiefs of the country.

There is no evidence that Apolo ever visited the capital during Mutesa's reign. However, there was considerable coming and going in the land, as chiefs were compelled to spend much time at the capital. Raiding parties came and went, news spread quickly, and there were few whose lives were not touched by what went on at the centre.

NOTES

[1] J. P. Thoonen, *Black Martyrs* (1942), p. 16.
[2] Information from Mr Gitta Kibuka, a relation of Apolo's.

[3] There are thirty-six traditional clans in Buganda. Each clan has two totems; it is taboo to kill, eat or wear the totem of your own clan. The Ngabi or Bushbuck clan is one of the royal clans. The Katinvuma totem is the seed of a climbing leguminous plant.

[4] Mutesa's predecessor.

[5] See J. Roscoe, *The Baganda* (1911); L. P. Mair, *An African People in the Twentieth century* (1934); H. B. Thomas and R. Scott, *Uganda* (1935).

[6] See A. B. Lloyd, *Apolo of the Pygmy Forest* (1923), p. 7.

[7] Apolo's diary.

[8] It would be tedious to recount in detail the complicated rites connected with twin ceremonies. They are described by Roscoe, *op. cit.*, pp. 64–73, and Mair, *op. cit.*, pp. 43–53.

[9] Correspondence with Bishop Kitching.

2

VISITORS FROM A WHITE LAND

The coming of the Arabs

ARAB slave-trading caravans from Zanzibar first arrived in Buganda in the days of Suna, Mutesa's predecessor,[1] having travelled up the west side of the lake from their depots in Tanganyika, bringing with them firearms and cloth. Further trade was encouraged, as Suna much desired these new and powerful weapons. But before he died he banned the traders from his country for ill-treating some of his subjects, and this prohibition continued into the early years of Mutesa's reign.

In 1862 two Englishmen, Speke and Grant, entered Buganda seeking for the source of the Nile. The strange fascination these intrepid and resolute white men must have had for Mutesa, as they sat and looked long at each other, was enhanced by the rumours that they came from a sacred land (whiteness is sacred in Buganda); but their prowess in the use of firearms, and the presentation of guns and powder and other articles of European manufacture to Mutesa probably impressed him even more and stimulated his desire to acquire more of such enviable possessions. From then on the acquisition of firearms was to become one of the main objects of his dealings with visitors from the outside world. The Arabs from Zanzibar were encouraged to trade at his court and he sent canoes across the lake to facilitate their transport, and his monopoly of this trade now helped him to increase his power over adjacent territories.[2]

At this time Arabs settled at Mutesa's court, among them

28

religious teachers, who began instructing the Kabaka and his principal chiefs in the faith of Islam. To some this religion made a real appeal and Mutesa himself embraced Islam. He may have done this in order to keep on good terms with the Sultan of Zanzibar, but his position was so strongly bound up with the pagan religion of his people that he could not abandon his old practices; he adopted the outward forms of the Islamic ritual in addition and commanded his subjects to do likewise. Apolo records, 'Our father first began to learn to read in the days of Mukabya from the Moslems. Kabaka Mutesa commanded all his chiefs and people to learn to read from the Moslems and to keep their fasts; we therefore fasted.'[3] But when some of his subjects embraced Islam seriously and showed independence of mind the Kabaka became alarmed and ordered a general massacre of all the converts. A large number were actually burnt alive. Some two or three hundred more managed to escape and join Arab caravans bound for Zanzibar. Apolo's family remained unharmed, doubtless because they were still living in Singo, far from the capital. This wholesale destruction is reputed to have taken place during the latter part of 1874, or early in 1875, before the arrival of H. M. Stanley's famous expedition at Mutesa's court.

Stanley and the C.M.S.

Apolo records: 'When I was about thirteen years old I heard that an English person had arrived in Buganda at the capital of Kabaka Mutesa and he too had brought reading. My father informed me thus "We have seen someone who comes from a white land". My mother thus argued about this "There are no such people, he has come from the sky, there we hear there are people with tails like cows". We said "In the sky there are no people", but she persisted "There are, we know it".'[4]

Stanley, the tough man of action, had been deeply influenced by the moral greatness of the lonely missionary Livingstone, whom he had met on the shores of Lake Tanganyika three years previously, and he saw in Mutesa the possible means of realizing Livingstone's great dream, whereby the slave trade in Africa could be suppressed by the opening up of the country to Christianity and civilization.

Thus he set about instructing Mutesa in the Christian religion, at the same time refuting the teaching of Islam and persuading him to agree that Christian missionaries should be sent to his kingdom. He wrote a famous letter to the *Daily Telegraph* on 14 April 1875, challenging Christian England to send a mission to Buganda. Mutesa and Stanley had been equally impressed with each other, and it may also be noted that Stanley assisted him successfully in a punitive expedition against the Bavuma.

Mutesa was undoubtedly interested in this new religious teaching, but it seems clear that his real motive for wanting white men at his court was to acquire their superior knowledge, for was it not they who made the weapons the Arabs brought into the country? They might also prove useful allies against the threatened annexation of his territory from the north by the agents of the Khedive of Egypt.

Before Stanley left in the early days of 1876, he translated extracts from the Bible into Kiswahili, with the help of a young servant of his, Dallington Scopion Muftaa (an ex-slave from Nyasaland and pupil of Universities' Mission in Zanzibar), whom he left at Mutesa's court to read the Bible for him. Dallington was to prove a useful interpreter to the first missionaries when they arrived the following year.

Apolo records: 'Then we heard the news that the Kabaka was reading after the manner of the white man. He had changed from Islam.' The missionaries for whom Stanley appealed had come: Lieutenant Shergold Smith, R.N., and the Rev. C. T. Wilson were sent by the Church Missionary Society and arrived on 30 June 1877, but Mutesa was disappointed with them, because they taught only religion and refused to make guns and powder.

They were given a site on which to build and were permitted to teach only at the court in the Kabaka's presence; their wisdom was not for all. Like all Mutesa's visitors the missionaries were virtual prisoners and could not move about without his consent. They were completely dependent upon his bounty or capricious neglect. Sometimes he sent abundant food, sometimes they starved.

After one month in Buganda, Shergold Smith left Wilson at

Mutesa's capital and returned to the south end of the lake to bring back supplies and another member of this first missionary party, but there the two missionaries met a tragic death. Wilson, now alone, made efforts to teach the Kabaka to read and preached at the court on Sundays, and before long, in defiance of the Kabaka's ban, a number of people came of their own accord to learn reading at Wilson's house. In January 1878 Wilson went south to meet Alexander Mackay whom he knew was endeavouring to join him.[5] In November they both returned to Rubaga (the hill upon which Mutesa's capital was at that time situated).

The personality of Mackay soon made itself felt. He was a man of singular ability and intelligence, a trained engineer and teacher— in every sense 'the pious, practical missionary' of Stanley's appeal, and at once his 'bold and intelligent appeal to the Scriptures seemed to have deeply impressed Mutesa, and his habit of referring all questions to the Word of God became in the end the chief factor in the mental and spiritual revolution which in the course of years passed over vast numbers of the Baganda'.[6] From this time those desirous of learning were allowed to attend the mission.

The two missionaries taught each Sunday in the Kabaka's court and daily instructed groups of chiefs and young men at the mission house.[7] Mackay was busy fitting up his workshop for iron work, with forge, anvil, lathe, vice, and grindstone, and these activities attracted a large crowd of boys. Here in this humble place, away from the clamour of the court, the Church was born in Uganda.

Mutesa was at first eager to learn and was strongly attracted to the teaching of the Christian book. 'Isa (Jesus)—was there anyone like him?' he said, and there were others also listening, who perhaps in their hearts sought after better things. However, even in these first days events occurred to bewilder and confuse the enquirers. Between February and June 1879 two parties of C.M.S. missionaries arrived at Mutesa's capital, most of whom decided not to stay, and what was far more perplexing, two parties of Roman Catholic priests of the Algerian White Fathers' Mission also arrived, who at once opposed the teaching of the Protestant mission.[8] 'How can I know what is right?' Mutesa asked. 'Every white man has a different religion.' Mackay recorded: 'It is with a very heavy heart that I think of the trouble now begun.'

For the remainder of 1879 Mutesa flirted with both Christian missions in turn and encouraged prolonged theological arguments between Mackay and the Moslems at court. The Moslems, of course, hated the missionaries for their bold denunciation of the slave-trade, and persuaded Mutesa that they were the vanguard of a conquering nation and must be expelled. All this time the old pagan religion was resentfully in the background, and in December of that year Mutesa openly returned to the old familiar things when he accepted the ministrations of the *lubale* of the lake to cure him of a long-standing illness. There followed a wholesale reversion to the old cruelties, and when the missionaries sent a letter of protest against a threatened mass human sacrifice to assist in Mutesa's recovery, they were banned from the court. For a time Mackay and those with him were virtually prisoners, and Mackay himself was in danger of his life.

For the next four years the life of both missions was precarious. The Roman Catholic mission left Buganda altogether in November 1882 and established themselves at the south end of the lake. Mackay's manual skill and willing service frequently softened the temper of Mutesa and helped to supply the necessities of life for himself and his two brethren. Moreover, Mutesa had gained prestige by having white men in his country and he had shown himself strong enough to control the opposing factions. From the missionaries' point of view, the Kabaka's divided mind on religion had at least shown his subjects that there was nothing sacrosanct about the old pagan religion. The teachings of the new religions were therefore scrutinized by some of the leaders and 'certain of the new moral and ethical ideas which were preached struck an answering chord in the minds of some Baganda, who sometimes wanted to know more.'[9] A revolution in the minds of the people had begun.

Steady work went on. Mackay seemed able to turn his hand to anything and many boys crowded about him as he worked, listening, watching, and talking to him. He also took his full share in the

Apolo in 1900

The first lady missionaries, Toro 1900

Toro landscape near Kabarole

Apolo's church at Mboga

teaching and translation work, and as soon as there was anything ready, he printed it on the small press belonging to the mission. By 1880 the *Mateka* or first reading book was completed. The enthusiasm of the people for reading when once the art was introduced was thus fed by the word of God, and in no other country has the Bible itself played so important a part in evangelization. The adherents of Christianity were from the beginning of the mission known as 'readers', and 'reading' was the mark of one who had at least begun to enquire about the Gospel. So it was that the first converts came from among the young boys who frequented the mission station, where they were taught to read and were 'carefully instructed'. Five were baptized in March 1882. Mackay writes of them: 'So far as we could judge of their answers, diligence and behaviour, they have resolutely made up their minds to become disciples of Jesus Christ, and face every risk which their confession may involve them in.'

For the last years of his life Mutesa was a sick man. It is said that he sent fewer people to the slaughter places, but it is recorded that thousands of slaves were sent to the coast instead.[10] Moreover, the occasion of Mutesa's death was not marked with the usual plundering and murder which in former times had followed the death of a Kabaka; he gave instructions that his body was to be buried, and not embalmed, and that no one was to be killed to accompany his ghost into the other world. There seems a possibility that the influence of Christian teaching had set up a new standard of right and wrong, acknowledged, perhaps, even by Mutesa himself. Likewise on the accession of Mwanga as Kabaka in October 1884 his brothers were not rounded up and burnt or starved to death as had been the custom in the past.

NOTES

[1] Sir John Gray, *Uganda Journal*, vol. 11 (1947), p. 82.

[2] It is interesting to note some of the rates of exchange for the Arab's merchandise. One musket—two slaves. One hundred percussion caps—one female slave. A *kanzu* with red embroidery was worth one woman or a big

tusk of ivory (valued at 18,000 cowrie shells). One pair of Arab sandals—one cow. A belt of beads with a scabbard—one woman or a slave or a tusk of ivory. Arab *joho*—six beautiful women. A red and black *kanzu*—four women. *Mackay of Uganda* by his Sister (1890), p. 105; Rev. B. Musoke Zimbe, *Buganda ne Kabaka* (1939), in MS. English translation, p. 25.

[3] Religious instruction, both Islamic and later Christian, was accompanied by learning to read the written word. Thus anyone being instructed in religion was called 'a reader'. Stanley records that Mutesa and the principal attendants at court had learnt to read and write Arabic. H. M. Stanley, *Through the Dark Continent* (1879), vol. i, chap. 15.

[4] It is not clear from Apolo's diary whether this white man was Stanley or one of the first C.M.S. missionaries who arrived in June 1877.

[5] Mackay was a member of the first Victoria Nyanza Mission party to enter the interior of East Africa, but due to ill health he soon had to return to the coast, where, however, the opportunity to master Kiswahili was to stand him in good stead later in his verbal battles at Mutesa's court. Of the eight men who composed this first party, only three finally reached Buganda —the Rev. C. T. Wilson, Shergold Smith, and Mackay.

[6] *Mackay of Uganda*, p. 145.

[7] They had brought with them the Gospels and Acts in Kiswahili (translated by Bishop Steere of the U.M.C.A. at Zanzibar).

[8] Eugene Stock, *History of the C.M.S.*, vol. iii (1899), p. 105.

[9] D. A. Low, *Religion and Society in Buganda 1875–1900* (1957), p. 2.

[10] C. T. Wilson and R. W. Felkin, *Uganda and the Egyptian Soudan* (1882), vol. i, pp. 189–90.

3

MARTYRS UNDER MWANGA

The great tribulation

APOLO records: 'After the death of Kabaka Mutesa, Mwanga became Kabaka (October 1884, he was only 18 years old). I then found people were beginning to read and the letters were very difficult. My brother fought in Mwanga's wars, and he learnt to read. The learners were very many in those days, also the number of Moslems were many too. My brother,[1] Mawanga was his name, was taught to read by Mackay. He told me all about it and tried to teach me. I went along to the place to read, but I refused to learn because of the difficulty of the letters in Kiswahili, so I left off learning to read.'

Mackay describes this: 'A great number, I may say about all, of the pages and storekeepers, etc., about the court are pupils, either of ours or the Papists.[2] Again and again I have seen the various store and other houses of the court literally converted into reading rooms . . . lads sitting in groups, or sprawling on the hay-covered floor, all reading; some the books of commandments and other texts; some the Church prayers, and others the Kiswahili New Testament. They are, besides, very eager to learn to write, and at all times are scribbling on boards, or any scraps of paper they can pick up . . . On Sunday the numbers that come far exceed our space, but outside is large enough for all, and when the inside of our chapel is filled with classes, others find a shady corner here and there out of doors.'[3]

It is related that Apolo spoke of Mackay saying: 'When I looked at the European, his eyes sparkled with kindness.'⁴ Although he found great difficulty with the reading it is unlikely that he could have left without hearing the story of Jesus Christ. What impression the story of Christ's coming among men must have had upon a 20-year-old lad of those times we do not know, but one thing seems certain, it was the memory of Mackay's kindness and quiet command of the situation that stayed with him and finally drew him to desire Christianity.

Apolo's brother was a 'soldier' in Mwanga's bodyguard. Mwanga surrounded himself with young men who served as pages and soldiers, known as the *Bainda*. Most of them would be quartered in the enclosures of the chiefs, where also Apolo would find lodging, probably serving his brother or else possibly employed at thatching or fence-making. Mwanga's new capital on Mengo (a hill adjoining Rubaga) was burnt to the ground twice in the first three years of his reign, and large numbers of people were conscripted to rebuild it. The young lad would have had ample opportunity for knowing all that went on in and around the capital.

In the days of Mwanga the old way of life began to disintegrate before the new and disturbing influences which were seeping into the heart of Africa. Mwanga was a weak and vicious youth who had not the strength to control his people as his father had done; he was surrounded by the rivalry and intrigue of his chiefs, who saw in Christian teaching a threat to their own power; he was harried by the Arabs, who persuaded him the missionaries' only object was to 'eat up his country'. These accusations were given point by rumours of the German annexation of the coast opposite Zanzibar and by Thomson's travels on the eastern borders of Busoga—the 'back door of Buganda', a route firmly closed to the outside world, as tradition had warned that Buganda would one day be conquered from the east. The new Christian doctrines also clashed with the customs of the Baganda and the old conservative chiefs fanned the smouldering fire of Mwanga's resentment towards the missionaries, whose influence over the youths at court greatly vexed him. Hence in a burst of fury against the English missionaries and those who consorted with them, three of the mission boys who had accompanied Mackay to the lake to see him off on one of his journeys to the south with mail were arrested and taken to the swamp near Natete, where they were dismembered and then burnt to death on 31 January 1885.

This was the beginning of the 'great tribulation'. Those who frequented the mission were threatened, and this precarious situation gave rise to the formation of the first church council, formed of men who were already the heads of household 'clusters' of converts, whose homes could be rallying points where worship and instruction might be carried on in times of trouble. The missionaries (Mackay, Ashe, and O'Flaherty) hastened to provide as much printed instruction as possible, and Mackay, with the help of some of the Christian converts, was also busy translating St Matthew's Gospel into Luganda.

In spite of the danger at this time, more people came to be taught and to seek baptism. The appeal of Christian teaching seemed to be real, and many of the converts had a great personal devotion to individual missionaries. Mackay especially won great love and respect in the nine years he spent in the country. His marvellous faith and his patient endurance of the disappointments and tragedies that drove lesser men from the field, made him like a strong enduring pillar supporting the infant Church through those first turbulent years.

In October of that year Mwanga struck again when he ordered the murder of Bishop Hannington. The Bishop had started for Uganda by the shorter route from Mombasa through Masailand before he received Mackay's warning not to come through 'the back door', and he was murdered with many of his porters when he reached the banks of the Nile in Busoga. Added to Mwanga's hatred and suspicion of the white men there was now also a guilty conscience which feared retaliation for this crime and prompted him to further outbursts of cruelty. Orders went out forbidding anyone to go near the mission on pain of death, the wisdom of the appointment of church 'elders', who could assemble a few Christians and others desirous of being taught with less danger than if they had attempted to visit the missionaries, was now evident.

Mwanga's hatred then turned towards the pages who befriended the missionaries, for he suspected them of giving away his secrets, and fifteen days after the murder of Hannington his favourite page Balikudembe Mukasa was put to death for daring to rebuke him for the Bishop's murder. Several other Christians were arrested, but were later set free.

For a while there was an uneasy lull and the work on St Matthew's Gospel progressed, each section translated being at once printed. Then in February 1886 Mwanga's whole palace was burnt to the ground, the fire originating in his powder store. Mwanga, fearing a rebellion, fled in terror and took up temporary residence at Munyonyo by the lake shore. He accused the white men of bewitching him and plotted to lure Mackay to a certain place by the lake shore and there have him murdered, but Mackay was warned and kept away. Mwanga's rising anger fed upon his awareness that his pages knew so much more than he did of a religion he did not want, and upon their growing independence of him and the refusal of many to join in the sexual perversions widely practised at the court.[5] Another factor was the independent behaviour of Princess Nalumansi, a baptized Roman Catholic, who burnt her ancestral relics and openly forsook the old superstitions. Anger led him to proclaim, 'The Christians are disobedient, and learn rebellion from the white man. I shall kill them all.'[6] Thus in May 1886 a great persecution of the Christians began, and no distinction was made between Roman Catholics and Protestants.

This was no unexpected crisis; from the days of Mutesa threats to exterminate the Christians had hung over the life of the converts, who embraced Christianity in the full knowledge that at any time they might be forced to disobey the Kabaka and imperil their lives. The fact that a number of lads of both missions openly and deliberately chose martyrdom is testimony enough to the reality of their religion. Yet also perhaps the underlying reverence for the office of the Kabaka may have made them the more submissive to death by his order.

Mwanga's grievances came to a head on 25 May 1886, when in a fit of uncontrollable passion he rampaged through his court at

Munyonyo venting his rage on all the pages and attendants present, who fortunately were not there in great numbers, as Mwanga's temporary enclosure was small, otherwise the numbers destroyed would have been greater. Those who were Christians were ordered to declare themselves, which they did without exception. Some of them were beaten, others condemned to be killed or shamefully mutilated. The following day there was a general arrest of 'readers', who were handed over to Mukajanga, the chief executioner, to be taken away and burnt to death at Namugongo, the traditional place of execution for court officials and those of royal blood. Other Christian leaders not present were sought out and arrested by the orders of Mwanga's ruthless *Katikiro* Mukasa,[7] whose hatred of Christianity was implacable. Yet others were the victims of parties of soldiers sent to raid the property of Christians.

It is generally agreed that thirty-two persons perished in the flames at Namugongo, and during the following months of persecution many unknown victims perished. Mackay wrote that 'many were speared or otherwise killed in an endeavour to capture them in various parts of the country'.[8]

Mackay holds on

Ashe wrote concerning this time: 'My overmastering feeling was that I would go and shake off the dust from my feet. "Not so," said Mackay, "there is work for you to do." As we set to work printing prayers and hymns and reading sheets . . . there was scarcely time for grief.'[9]

'Our people venture,' wrote Mackay, 'a few of them, to come to me every evening after dark. Those . . . marked out for execution, and particularly sought after, dare only come about midnight. I give them a little instruction and comfort, and we pray together. Several of them I cannot refuse to help materially, as they are reduced to beggary, and are in want.'

The missionaries tried to withdraw from the country for a time in the hope of removing the suspicions against them and against those who accepted their teaching. In August 1886 Ashe was allowed to go, but Mackay was kept back as a hostage. He was not permitted to go far from home and was jealously watched and remained alone for another year, the Christians visiting him secretly. He tried to overcome Mwanga's fears by doing various kinds of work for him, such as erecting an enormous flag staff in the *lubiri*; he went quietly on with his teaching, carpentry, and weaving, and made a great effort to complete St Matthew.

The Christians of both missions 'no longer frequented the court, with the exception of those who had been pardoned. Some in fact had been pardoned because they rendered Mwanga great service, as for instance Matthew Kisule, his gunsmith. Others had been pardoned, but first mutilated'.[10] An able young man, Honorat Nyonyintono, a Roman Catholic convert, held the chieftainship of *Kisalosalo*,[11] and Apolo Kagwa, a C.M.S. convert, was given the office of *Muwanika*;[12] both of these young men had suffered grievously at the hands of Mwanga during the persecution.

However, Mwanga's desire to rid himself of the converts in hiding still smouldered; he tried a ruse to lure the Christians out of hiding by promising them estates, and one, Jamari Muzeyi, came out and was seized and secretly murdered. Another great fire destroyed Mwanga's new enclosure on 22 February 1887 and was looked upon as judgement from heaven for Jamari's murder; yet it was also rumoured that Mwanga was threatening another great slaughter of Christians, but the *Katikiro* and the *Namasole*[13] advised forbearance, as the young men were the chief strength of the country.

About this time the fickle Kabaka took up the Moslem religion and ordered all his *Bainda* to read the Koran. When many of them refused he complained that they compelled him ever to be killing them, so that people would call him a madman.

A paragraph in Apolo's diary may well fit in here. 'We were fighting Kigaju, and it was while I was there that I saw a difference between the Moslems and the Christians. The Moslems would not eat meat killed by uncircumcised Baganda, but the Christians did not have this scruple. It was then that I knew there was a God in heaven and refused to associate myself with the Moslems.'

It was probably at this time that Apolo and his brother joined the pagan army led by *Pokino* Tebukoza; for he later states 'we were known as the pagan army'. It would not have been safe openly to join the Christians at this time. In May 1887 Mwanga had declared war against Kabarega, the powerful Mukama of Bunyoro, and he threatened that if the Christians did not fight they would be burnt. However, Kabarega on this occasion sued for peace and the Baganda army diverted its energies to raiding south-west in Buddu.

'Upon reaching Nateta (in Buddu) Mwanga sent out *Pokino* Kyambalango Tebukoza to fight Kigaju Bukyusa Buzinja' (a Muhuma chief of Kiziba).[14] No doubt Apolo and his brother played their part in killing and plundering. It appears that Mwanga was at the time alienating his old chiefs by taking from them their prowess and success in war.

When not raiding the soldiers were employed on fence-building in the Kabaka's enclosure. After the last great fire of February 1887, the chiefs were turned out to rebuild the capital, and very heavy fines of women and cattle were imposed upon those who failed to obey the command.

Meanwhile the Arabs renewed their accusation against Mackay as a political agent, and the news that H. M. Stanley's Emin Relief Expedition was approaching from the Congo lent colour to their lies. Mwanga agreed to send Mackay away, but insisted on his place being taken by the Rev. E. C. Gordon, who was at Msalala at the south of the lake.[15] This spoiled the plan of the Arabs, who had hoped to plunder the mission station after Mackay's departure. Before leaving, Mackay summoned the church council and made provision for the relief of Christians in distress. Every copy of St Matthew in Luganda was bought up. Mackay left Buganda on 21 July 1887, and Gordon arrived with the returning boat. The church leaders, still in hiding, came by stealth and helped Gordon take over the work. 'Readers' continued to come. There was another scare, but nothing came of it and the year passed away peacefully. In April 1888 the Rev. R. H. Walker joined Gordon.

The tyrant overthrown

Mwanga was becoming increasingly disliked by his subjects. His *Bainda* plundered without restraint. Ham Mukasa, who was one of the Kabaka's pages, records that Mwanga 'kept a crowd of lads of the worst sort about him—they used to get drunk by smoking bhang—and they tried to teach me other sins'.[16]

Insubordination amongst his subjects led Mwanga to threaten reprisals. The opposition of the Christian and Moslem parties began to stiffen and finally they joined forces to depose Mwanga, who fled to the south end of the lake and took refuge at the Arab settlement of Magu. Mutesa's eldest son Kiwewa, contrary to tradition which debarred the eldest son from succeeding his father, was made Kabaka. The Moslems favoured another man, Kalema, but he was at the time living far from the capital.

NOTES

[1] This may have been one of Apolo's two elder brothers; the fact that he was a Moslem suggests that he was, but all the men of the same generation in a clan are called brother.

[2] Mwanga, prompted by influential Roman Catholic converts at court, invited the French priests back to Buganda in July 1885. During their absence their converts had continued diligently to teach their religion and the Church had grown.

[3] Sarah G. Stock, *The Story of Uganda and the Victoria Nyanza Mission* (1892), pp. 111–12.

[4] G. R. Katongole, *Apolo Kivebulaya owe Mbooga* (1952), pp. 4–5.

[5] Sodomy was introduced by the Arabs in Mutesa's reign.

[6] *Mackay of Uganda*, p. 276.

[7] Chief Minister.

[8] This account of the Baganda Martyrs is based upon *African Holocaust* (1962) by J. F. Faupel; and H. B. Thomas, 'The Baganda Martyrs, 1885–1887', *Uganda Journal*, vol. 15 (1951), pp. 90–91.

[9] *Mackay of Uganda*, pp. 308–9. Ashe and Mackay were now alone; O'Flaherty had left in December 1885.

[10] J. P. Thoonen, *Black Martyrs* (1942), p. 265.

[11] Major-domo.

[12] Chief storekeeper.

[13] Queen Mother.

[14] Sir Apolo Kagwa, *Basekabaka be Buganda* (1927), p. 142.

[15] The C.M.S. has established a number of mission stations between the coast and the south end of Lake Victoria. Msalala was little more than a depot for Uganda, although the missionaries destined for Uganda had attempted mission work there, but so rapacious was the chief of the area that when Mackay returned there he evacuated the station, which was moved to Usambiro in the territory of a more friendly chief.

[16] See note 3 in chapter 6.

4

THE CHRISTIANS SEIZE POWER

The exiles in Ankole

THE uneasy alliance between Christians and Moslems lasted
rather less than a month. The Moslem party, dissatisfied
with its share of chieftainships and estates, and encouraged by the
Arabs, soon found a pretext for attacking the Christians, who,
taken by surprise, had to fight for their lives and were defeated.
They then fled westwards with their leaders Honorat Nyonyintono
and Apolo Kagwa, and finally took refuge in Ankole, where Ntare,
the Mugabe,[1] gave them five tusks of ivory, thirty to forty head
of cattle and a number of villages in Kabula on the frontier of
Ankole.

Meanwhile the Moslems, too preoccupied to pursue them, were
attacking and pillaging the missions. The missionaries[2] were taken
prisoner, despoiled of almost all they possessed, and together with
two servants and twenty-two orphans were taken to Munyonyo
and thrust on board the C.M.S. vessel *Eleanor*. After many hard-
ships they reached the south end of the lake.

The helpless and fearful Kiwewa resisted the Moslem design to
circumcise him by force and fled to Singo, where he was captured.
Later he was cruelly put to death. In his place the Moslems proclaimed Kalema as Kabaka. He was ready to satisfy in full all the
demands of the Arabs and the Moslem party and to enforce Islam
on all his subjects, including the pagans, who were by far the largest
section of the population.[3]

It is recorded that Apolo was at the capital at this time and as

44

he was known as a Moslem he was forced to join their army. *Pokino* Tebukoza, leader of the pagan army, had gone over to the Moslems, and it is likely that many of his followers went with him, including Apolo and his brother.[4] The Moslems raided the country and performed deeds of sickening cruelty, setting huts on fire after having tied the men, women, and children to the surrounding banana trees, so that in the heat of the burning huts they began to burst like dried maize being roasted.[5]

Apolo witnessed these things. 'He was grieved to the heart by the great cruelty to his people. Although he was known as a Moslem, his heart was not in it. All the time he remembered the "love" of that European (Mackay) and felt ashamed that he was on the side of those who were persecuting the missionaries' followers. On one occasion he and his companions besieged a village and killed many people and as their custom was, they began burning the people. The smell filled the whole village. Apolo's revulsion increased, he could see no love in the Moslem religion and so he resolved to run away.'[6] Like many others, he and his brother made their way to Ankole, where they joined the Protestant Christians. 'It was then that I really began to be friends with the "readers". It was then I began to pray, from seeing my fellows pray. I learnt to pray before I could read.'[7]

After four or five months the number of fugitives in Ankole had grown enormously. Apolo Kagwa, the leader of the Protestants, now had under his command a thousand men armed with guns, besides women and children, many of them starving. The Christian forces repaid the Mugabe's generosity by raiding into Buganda and Rwanda, bringing back cattle which they presented to Ntare. In addition they bridged rivers and performed works of public utility to prove their gratitude. Unfortunately mutual differences, jealousies, and suspicions were already beginning to prevent the Protestant and Roman Catholic sections from pulling together.

Mwanga restored by 'Christian' arms

Meanwhile Mwanga had been fleeced of all he possessed by the Arabs at Magu. He then escaped by night to Bukumbi, where the

45

White Fathers had established a mission, and begged their forgiveness and hospitality. When this news reached the Christians in Ankole, who were planning to regain control of their country, they sought to legitimize their plans by proposing to restore Mwanga once more. Therefore a deputation of both Protestants and Roman Catholics was sent to Usambiro and Bukumbi. Mackay declined to assist, as he felt that any such attempt to restore Mwanga to his throne by force of arms would expose all missionaries in Central Africa to serious danger. However, the Roman Catholic priests lent their support, and Charles Stokes, and ex-C.M.S.-missionary turned trader, agreed to lend his boat and supply arms. Then on 29 April, 'Mwanga and I then started', says Stokes, 'for Buganda in my boat and about forty guns, principally Le Gras and Sniders, and 500 to 600 rounds of ammunition. On arrival at our first point, Buddu, many thousand fighting men joined Mwanga's standard, and after waiting about ten days the Christians, about 800 strong, joined us.'[8]

They found that the Christians had already been in action and had suffered heavy losses, including the Roman Catholic leader Nyonyintono. On hearing of Mwanga's arrival at Dumu the Moslem party advanced in force on his camp. Fortunately Stokes was at hand with his boat and a fleet of canoes and was able to take Mwanga and his (Catholic) party off to the Sese Islands,[9] while the remainder of the Christians retired towards Ankole. Before returning to the south to bring up more powder and ammunition, Stokes landed Mwanga and his party on the small island of Bulingugwe in Murchison Bay, close to the landing place at Munyonyo, which was about two hours' walk from Rubaga.

Kalema was becoming increasingly unpopular with the pagan element for his efforts to force Islam upon them and for the cruel manner in which he had killed Kiwewa.[10] To add to his discomfort he was also running short of ammunition, and the destruction of two Arab dhows from Magu laden with arms and ammunition, by a small contigent of Mwanga's army, marked the turning-point of the war.

Indecisive fighting had continued in Buddu, and the Christians

46

had again retreated into Ankole. However, a pagan force now attacked the Moslems, who had to withdraw to the capital. Mwanga, with Stokes's aid, had sent a letter to the Imperial British East Africa Company's expedition under Frederick Jackson, known to be making its way through Masailand to Lake Victoria. It begged them 'to be good enough to put me on my throne. I will give you plenty of ivory and you may do any trade in Buganda and all you like in the country under me'. He also sent messengers to seek aid from Stanley, now making his way through Ankole, and he wrote to Mackay and Mgr Livinhac imploring their aid.[11]

Thus two missionaries from the Roman Catholic mission, Fathers Lourdel and Denoit, accompanied Stokes, who was returning to Mwanga's assistance, while Cyril Gordon and Robert Walker of the C.M.S. followed Stokes's vessel in canoes. (Mackay was busy trying to complete a steam launch for the mission, and so delayed his hoped-for return to Buganda.) 'All along the coast were fires which had been started by Kalema's people to destroy the houses and plantations of their opponents.'[12] They reached Bulingugwe on 14 September, where conditions of overcrowding on this tiny island had led to both famine and disease; the ministrations of the missionaries were sorely needed, and not least in quietening the hostile feelings between the Roman Catholic and Protestant factions. The widening rift between them might otherwise have wrecked their chances against Kalema.

The Christian forces in Ankole were now fighting their way towards the capital, and assisted by men and arms from Mwanga's contingent, finally drove the Moslems out of Mengo, who, with Kalema, took refuge in Singo.

On 11 October 1889 Mwanga entered the capital, now reduced to ruins and ashes. Gardens were overgrown, and both missions obliterated; swarms of vultures were swooping down on corpses which nobody troubled to bury.[13] The peasants, armed with spears, plundered what was left.

Gordon records: 'The next few days were occupied with the business of the division of the country among the victors. The whole land has been divided between the two bodies of Christians.

47

The Protestants and Roman Catholics have taken up all the chief-tainships, dividing the land attached to these chieftainships equally among themselves. The numerous heathen party has hardly got anything at all, but had still less when the Muhammadans were in power.'[14]

However, Kalema was still a power in the land. He tried to enter Bunyoro, but was refused entry, so he stationed himself on the border. Then, assisted by Kabarega, he attacked Singo. Apolo Kagwa was sent to repulse him, but Kagwa's force was defeated and retreated to Mengo with Kalema hard on his heels. Mwanga and the missionaries fled once more to Bulingugwe island and Kalema reoccupied Mengo with a strong force of Banyoro. Mwanga appealed again to Jackson for help. His forces were now dispersed; religious discord, plague, and starvation added to the chaos and loss. However, the arrival of Stokes's boat at the end of January 1890 with guns and powder encouraged the Christians to rally again,[15] and finally, in February, the combined Christian forces took the capital and drove the Moslems into Bunyoro, where Kalema died of smallpox in April. Mwanga returned to his throne once again, no longer as the despotic symbol of the nation's unity, but merely as the leader of a faction. The names Protestant, Roman Catholic and Moslem had now taken on a strongly political significance, and the resulting discord between these factions found the country in a very precarious state when Captain F. D. Lugard of the Imperial British East Africa Company arrived to offer Mwanga the Company's protection in December 1890.

NOTES

[1] King of Ankole.

[2] Messrs Gordon and Walker of the C.M.S., Léon Livinhac (Vicar Apostolic), Fathers Siméon Lourdel and Denoit, and a lay brother, Amans.

[3] Sir John Gray in *Uganda Journal*, vol. 14 (1950), pp. 27–28.

[4] G. R. Katongole, *Apolo Kivebulaya owe Mbooga*, p. 4; A. B. Lloyd, *Apolo of the Pygmy Forest*, p. 9.

[5] This performance was known as *okwokya emberenge* (dried maize burning). Musoke Zimbe, *Buganda ne Kabaka*, p. 241.

Apolo with a Pygmy chief

'How beautiful are the feet of them that preach the gospel of peace'

[6] Katongole, *op. cit.*, pp. 4–5.

[7] Apolo's diary.

[8] Gray, *op. cit.*, p. 33.

[9] These islands were centres of the *lubale* worship. Thus the Basese were staunch supporters of the old pagan cults, and resented Kalema's attempts to force Islam upon them. The navigation of the lake was almost entirely in their hands, and their support was an important factor in Mwanga's favour.

[10] Disquieted by the unexpected resistance of the Christians and their readiness to support Mwanga, Kalema also feared that other members of the royal family might try to oust him from his position. He therefore had thirty princes and princesses burnt to death, including two infant sons of Mwanga. Kiwewa was first starved of both food and water for seven days before being shot and his body burned. Sir Apolo Kagwa writes: 'The manner of killing him was not a fit manner in which to kill a king . . .' Gray, *op. cit.*, pp. 35–36.

[11] *Ibid.*, p. 41.

[12] *Ibid.*, p. 42.

[13] Lourdel's diary. *Ibid.*, p. 45.

[14] Rev. E. C. Gordon, letter to Col. Euan-Smith, 25 October 1889. *Ibid.*, p. 46.

[15] Stokes himself was now on his way to Zanzibar.

5

THE PACIFICATION OF UGANDA

Civil war and spiritual awakening

'AFTER we had driven off the Moslems,' Apolo tells us in his diary, 'I began to learn to read. The Moslems went to Bunyoro. The Christians were then in possession of Buganda. My brother had told me about the differences between the Protestants and Roman Catholics and Moslems. Then I decided to "read" as a Protestant. My brother, however, decided to remain a Moslem, but he found it difficult! He did, however, get a small reading book which helped me to read. I read with my people at home.'

With the country so lately ravaged by civil war, Singo had become largely deserted. Apolo's parents had moved from Singo to settle on the clan lands in the county of Kyadondo, and to begin with they lived at a place called Kiinda, about eight miles from Mengo.[1]

'After a time some bhang-smokers came and taught me to smoke,[2] so I left off learning to read and became a bhang-smoker. Then the English built a church near my home. I sometimes found the readers at the home of Mr Kitakule.[3] Kitakule gathered many young "readers" in his home for instruction and fellowship. I tried to persevere. I gave up bhang-smoking and began to read the Gospel and at that time I really understood and was recognized as understanding. Then I left the company of the bhang-smokers.'

Apolo was probably once again employed on thatching buildings in the devastated capital. Kabaka Mwanga was one day inspecting the work when he 'noticed I was wearing clothes like the Nubians, then the Kabaka said "*Mulongo* (the twin) is a Nubian?". From that day I was known as the Nubian—*Omunubi*!' The Sudanese soldiers, called by the Baganda, Banubi, wore calico trousers and tunics. These were possibly exchanged for food and other commodities. Apolo must have acquired such a uniform from the Sudanese soldiers recently come into the country with Lugard and Williams. Apolo's skin, like that of the Nubians, was very dark; he also wore a small piece of cloth, turban fashion on his head; a mode of head-gear introduced by the Arabs and widely worn. Even for a while after he had been baptized Apolo wore this turban, a relic of his Moslem days. As we shall see later, he had a taste for nice clothes.

'When the English called for soldiers they would often refuse me on account of my Nubian dress,' Apolo's diary continues. 'The *Katikiro* Apolo Kagwa told them I was not a Nubian, although I dressed like one. They then agreed. As I had this desire to become a Christian, I asked that as I was learning to read I might be allowed to have a day off a week to continue my study.'

In an attempt to keep the peace in the faction-ridden capital, Lugard tried the experiment of a local police force, drawn from the two Christian parties, to patrol the roads of the capital; their duties were to check all disturbances and prevent men carrying arms. This little force came into being about 16 March 1891 and 'consisted of a patrol of three Protestants and three Roman Catholics with six Zanzibaris and three Sudanese. These fifteen men went out at 8 a.m. and patrolled the roads about Mengo, returning about noon, and being relieved by a similar body . . . the Waganda being dressed in scarlet calico jackets so as to be easily recognizable . . . However, although great pains were taken with this attempt at a police force, it never succeeded, for the Waganda were entirely unadapted by nature and temperament to such routine work'.[4] Some months later, while Captain Lugard was away in western Uganda, Captain Williams disbanded the force.

However, Apolo's work of 'being a soldier' had not ended, for the war drums still beat out their challenge. The country was in a ferment; the four hostile camps, consisting of the two Christian parties, the Moslems and the pagan Futabhangi,[5] were perhaps

51

unconsciously struggling to replace the old autocratic control. Provocations, threats, and outrages continued, and small contingents of Protestant forces assisted the Europeans to quell these outbursts. Finally the struggle between the Roman Catholics and Protestants came to a climax in the Battle of Mengo in January 1892, when the attacking Roman Catholics were driven off by the Protestants aided by Captain Lugard, who with great firmness and impartiality finally persuaded the warring factions to agree to peace and a territorial settlement. However, it merely needed the removal of the British control for the uneasy peace once more to break down.

In spite of the unsettled state of the country, Christian teaching spread like a flood. No doubt political rivalry acted as a stimulus, but 'the one cry was for books and instruction'.[6] George Pilkington, who came with the party of missionaries led by Bishop Tucker in December 1890, continued where Mackay had left off translating the Bible into Luganda. (Mackay had died at Usambiro in February of that same year). This heavy task Pilkington completed before he was killed in the Sudanese rebellion in December 1897.

Bishop Tucker speaks of the groups of eager enquirers, scattered about in the church, each taught by a man who was himself at other times in the day an eager learner in a more advanced group. It was clear to the Bishop 'that if Africa is to be won for Christ it must be done by the African himself'. Already he had set aside a number of church leaders as lay readers who were the forerunners of the African ministry, which within eighteen years was numbering thirty-two priests and deacons and some 2,500 lay workers 'scattered throughout the land'. It is significant that in April 1893 forty Christian chiefs gave freedom to their slaves, even in the teeth of the Kabaka's disapproval.

A deepening of the life of the growing Church came towards the end of 1893, when a spiritual revival swept through its ranks which gave new impulse to ordinary Christians to offer themselves as evangelists. The Church began to reach out into the country districts. Apolo records: 'At that time I was reading St Matthew's Gospel and I was enjoying it very much, especially Chapter 5 v. 13.

These were the chapters that had most influence on my becoming a Christian and to leave my work of being a soldier.'

Then in March 1893 Apolo was 'chosen to help dig the road from Kampala to Toro'. It is recorded that when Sir Gerald Portal went to see the Kabaka about making the road to Toro, the Kabaka complained that the Roman Catholics and Moslems would not do their share.[7] Thus it fell to the Protestant chiefs to supply labour for this task. The former broad straight roads of the country had long been neglected and almost obliterated by the rank growth of grass and bush. This road to the west was now to be used by Major Roddy Owen, who was ordered to withdraw the Sudanese garrisons from the forts where Lugard had placed them to protect the Toro border against raiding Banyoro. The Sudanese had, however, begun ravaging the country they had been left to protect and were therefore to be withdrawn.

Apolo refers to this road-making: 'In all the work I was given it was found that I was strong and worked hard, the chiefs praised me. I was also praised because I did not play around with the other workers. After I had been working on the road for some time we had got as far as Mityana.'

The work consisted mostly of clearing the overgrown paths which ran straight up and down the hills without regard for gradients; rough causeways were built of felled trees and earth over the intervening swamps, but usually the traveller had to wade knee- or waist-deep through these. According to Colvile the work on this road to Mityana did not appear to have been very effective,[8] probably because the road gangs were soon overtaken by waves of fleeing Moslems (the First Sudanese Mutiny and rebellion of Moslem Baganda of June 1893) pursued once again by the 'Christian' armies to the border of Toro, where they came under the command of Major Owen, who subsequently returned them to the capital.

The campaign against Kabarega

Before long, however, the war drums were again sounding, and all the able-bodied men were called to the capital to muster for an onslaught against Kabarega of Bunyoro. Kabarega's armies were raiding Busoga and had again overrun Toro, now bereft of its Sudanese garrisons, and its young ruler, the Mukama Kasagama[9] had taken refuge in the Ruwenzori mountains. Kabarega was reputed to have 8,000 guns and 20,000 spearmen.[10]

If peace was to be established at all in Uganda, clearly Kabarega must be dealt with. Also, British interests in the Nile Basin were threatened by a suspected Belgian advance. Therefore a campaign to the west was opportune. It was launched by Colonel Colvile, the newly arrived British Commissioner.

By the middle of December the British-led Sudanese troops and the hordes of Baganda armed with spears and muskets started for the frontier.[11] This vast army pitched camp at a village south of the Kafu river. The missionary George Pilkington accompanied the Baganda contingent, hoping to meet people who never came near the capital. 'I have preached to great crowds four times, numbering from 1,000 to 2,000.'[12] It is probable that enquirers like Apolo were constantly about him. Lieutenant Villiers, speaking of Pilkington's presence with the Baganda army, remarks that it was 'the cause of their abandoning all their former ideas of warfare, and behaving as well as civilized troops'.[13] It was rather an optimistic observation, hardly borne out by other accounts, but no doubt a different standard of behaviour in warfare was for the first time put before them, and some doubtless did respond.

On 29 December 1893 the army crossed the Kafu and advanced on Kabarega's capital at Mparo, only to find it in ashes, Kabarega having retired to the fastnesses of the Budongo forest. Apolo mentions that 'we fought Kabagambe'. Kabagambe was one of Kabarega's chiefs—perhaps leading a rearguard action.

The hopelessness of catching Kabarega in the forest was obvious. His power could only be broken by the occupation of his country; Colvile therefore decided to build a chain of forts from Kibiro on Lake Albert to the Kafu, to be garrisoned by the Sudanese, thus cutting Bunyoro in half at its narrowest point and confining Kabarega to the northern part of his kingdom; then to encircle him in his forest by occupying Magungo, the only food district to the north, while the Baganda were persuaded to remain on the southern fringe of the forest to patrol the edges. Once again they built a vast camp and Pilkington set up a church where he and the lay readers who were with him held services, and 'outdoor meetings were held nightly'.[14]

After a successful skirmish against Kabarega, the Baganda were anxious to turn homeward, as smallpox had broken out in their ranks and food was scarce. By the middle of February the forts were established and the Baganda dispersed to their homes. Colvile himself was ready to withdraw and Major Thruston was left to command the garrisons in occupied Bunyoro. This he did for another year. With his small Sudanese force he captured the stronghold of Masaja Mkuru and repulsed a big attack by Kabarega against Hoima fort. He finally destroyed Kabarega's camp at Mashudi, and the latter fled to the lands beyond the Nile, never again to return.

The occupation of Toro

Before leaving Bunyoro, Colvile sent off a small expedition under the command of Major Roddy Owen 'accompanied by Lieutenant Villiers, 38 Sudanese and 47 Swahilis, with orders to restore confidence in Toro, establish a post on the Albert Edward Lake, and form the confederacy of friendly southern Unyoro chiefs'.[15] It appears that Apolo attached himself to this expedition, for he says, 'there in Toro I was well thought of'. He may have been engaged as a porter, or perhaps to help forage for food or cut undergrowth to clear paths through the wild country between Hoima and Fort Gerry in Toro.

It was a perilous journey through hostile country; the marching column had to be on the alert against attacks from an elusive enemy seldom visible in the long grass and thick bush. Roddy Owen described it: 'It was not until 26 February, after a most anxious march, that a camp between the old forts 1 and 2 was reached. The view from this camp over the rich Toro country was very beautiful. In front lay the grand rolling downs leading up to the Toro mountains, and far above these, in distance beyond distance, like an immense barrier between the Congo and Uganda, rose the snow-capped peaks of the Ruwenzori range.'[16]

On 3 March 1894 Major Owen made a treaty with Kasagama on behalf of the British Government. In return for British protection Kasagama agreed to keep peace between his country and Great Britain, and to cede no territory to any foreign power without Britain's consent. He also promised to abolish slave trading and raiding, to give up deserters with their guns and ammunition, and to punish any of his people discovered buying ammunition or guns from any British Government servants. In addition he was to pay the Government forty *frasila* of ivory (1 *frasila*, 36 lb. of ivory, was worth £20) annually, and to supply the garrisons with food.[17]

Garrisons were now allotted to Fort George at the Katwe salt lake and Fort Gerry, the latter to protect Kasagama's headquarters at Kabarole. Fort Gerry was named after Sir Gerald Portal (Her Majesty's first Commissioner to Uganda). The town that grew up there later was renamed Fort Portal. These garrisons were small, but would be a 'nucleus round which the tribesmen might collect to repel any inroad of Manyuema from the west',[18] while the new forts in Bunyoro would protect them from invasion from the north. 'In token of their new position they were given the British Flag.'[19]

By slow marches Owen and his men made their way back to Kampala; the forts he had visited in the previous year were overgrown and the paths so frequently trodden now hidden and impassable.

Apolo's experiences during these months of campaign in Bunyoro and Toro can only be left to surmise, but one thing is likely: he came in contact with Europeans of outstanding character. In particular he met the ardent missionary Pilkington, full of zeal and love for the people amongst whom he went to point a way to God, and Major Roddy Owen, an intrepid and energetic leader of men. Perhaps some impress of these men's influence was left upon him.

NOTES

[1] Information from Ruben Kakonge.

[2] Indian hemp, first brought into the country by the Arab traders. Mackay in a letter to the C.M.S. (29 September 1885) refers to Kabaka Mwanga's addiction to bhang-smoking. 'I believe that it induces a sensation of temporary delirium, and, if persevered in, causes a peculiar insanity.' See Sir John Gray in *Uganda Journal*, vol. 13 (1949), p. 7.

[3] Henry Wright Duta Kitakule was a leading Christian, and a member of the first church council of 1885. He was attacked in the persecution of 1886, but escaped to his family estates in Bulemezi and changed his name to Kitakule. He became a lay reader in 1891, a deacon in 1893, and was priested in 1896. He was George Pilkington's principal assistant in translating the Bible into Luganda, and served at Namirembe until he died in 1913. At the time Apolo refers to him Kitakule lived on the flanks of Namirembe hill near Mengo. This hill, the most prominent of the many hills surrounding the capital, had recently been occupied by the C.M.S. mission, and upon its summit a large thatched church was being built.

[4] F. J. D. Lugard, *The Rise of our East African Empire* (1893), vol. ii, pp 94–95, 105–6.

[5] 'Bhang-smokers.' The pagan party took this name because bhang-smoking was forbidden by Christians.

[6] A. R. Tucker, *Eighteen Years in Uganda and East Africa* (1911), p. 48.

[7] Sir Gerald Portal, *The British Mission to Uganda in 1893* (1894), p. 340.

[8] Col. Sir H. Colvile, *The Land of the Nile Springs* (1895), pp. 84–85, 227–28.

[9] The Mukama Kasagama Kyebambe was the third incumbent of the throne of Toro, a small kingdom which had once been part of Bunyoro and had hived off under an independent ruler in the first half of the nineteenth century. During Kasagama's childhood he and his family had been driven out of Toro by Kabarega's invading armies. He had finally found refuge with a kinsman in Buddu. When in 1891 Lugard marched west to enlist the Sudanese troops left by Emin Pasha in Equatoria, Kasagama came forward with his claims to the throne of Toro. Lugard established him as the rightful ruler of Toro and at the same time placed a number of Sudanese garrisons astride the Toro-Bunyoro frontier to prevent further invasions.

[10] Colvile, *op. cit.*, p. 71.

[11] Eight Europeans commanded the 400 Sudanese, while Semei Kakunguru led about 14,000 Baganda warriors. Major Thruston remarked that the muskets in the hands of the inexperienced Baganda were far less dangerous weapons than poisoned arrows and spears. A. B. Thruston, *African Incidents* (1900), p. 153.

[12] Harford-Battersby, *Pilkington of Uganda* (1898), p. 230.

[13] *Ibid.*, p. 230.

[14] Thruston, *op. cit.*, p. 149.

[15] Colvile, *op. cit.*, p. 214.

[16] Bovill and Askwith, *Roddy Owen—A Memoir* (1897), pp. 169–70.

[17] Entebbe MSS. Inward, 1894: Treaty made near Fort Gerry in Toro, in Central Africa, 3 March 1894.

[18] After Lugard had withdrawn the Sudanese from Kavalli's, west of Lake Albert, the place was occupied by Manyuema slave hunters, who also established themselves in a stockaded position west of the Semliki river at the southern end of Ruwenzori, from where they raided southern Toro. These Manyuema traded slaves with the Arab slavers operating in the Congo. Colvile, *op. cit.*, p. 230.

[19] Bovill and Askwith, *op. cit.*, pp. 170–1.

Part Two

A MAN OF GOD

6

THE WORK OF AN EVANGELIST

The planting of the Church in Toro

WHEN Apolo returned from the expedition to Toro he wished to be instructed for baptism: 'I still had a great longing to become a man of God. In 1894 I began to read for baptism with all my strength. I hated the world and the works of it. I always read "Go ye into all the world and preach the Gospel". At that time my father had chosen a bride for me. I read with her, but she died.'[1] In later years Apolo looked upon this as a providential release. He never took a wife. His work in lands far from his home would have made life hard for a woman of his own people.

'Then I went to the C.M.S. missionaries, and told them I wanted to be baptized. They wanted to know if I had finished studying the catechism; it was seen that I knew all about it. Then I was sent off to find my witnesses (god-parents). The only women I knew were of bad reputation, therefore, I had two men as witnesses.' He was baptized on 27 January 1895, and took the name Apollos, having in mind the passage: 'and being fervent in the spirit, he spake and taught diligently the things of the Lord' (Acts 18.25). We shall see how completely his life fulfilled these words.

'In June 1895 I asked that I might become a teacher.[2] I then did some more reading at Namirembe and from time to time I was sent to preach the Gospel to the children in the villages around the town.' It is said that the children teased him because of his quaint appearance. He was still wearing his Nubian trousers and jacket, which marked him out from the others, since the long white kanzu

61

was now being worn by all men of substance. He also walked with great rapidity as he went about with his bag of books, a somewhat comic figure.

He came to town on Saturdays and stayed at the enclosure of Ham Mukasa[3] so as to be able to attend the Sunday services at Namirembe. 'One day when I was in church, some teachers who had come from Toro said they badly needed more teachers. I went at once to Roscoe, and explained that I wanted to go to Toro. I was asked for a sponsor who knew me well, so I fetched Ham Mukasa. It was first agreed that I should be sent to Bunyoro, but then they sent me to Toro in September 1895.'

Two teachers had gone to Toro in 1894 at the request of the Mukama Kasagama, who had himself received Christian instruction during his exile in Buddu. Here he had stayed with a kinsman, Yafeti (Japheth) Byakweyamba, who had been captured long ago by Mutesa's armies and detained at the court of Buganda, where he had come under the influence of the Protestant missionaries. In later years he was given the chieftainship of Kitanda in Buddu. When Lugard returned with Kasagama to Toro, Byakweyamba accompanied him and received the chieftainship of Mwenge. It was through his efforts that the first two teachers, Marko Lwimbazi and Petero Nsubuga, came to Toro.

Then in September 1895 came Apolo Kivebulaya and another teacher, Sedulaka (Shadrach) Zabunamakwata. It will be noticed that Apolo has acquired yet another name, 'Kivebulaya', meaning literally 'the thing from England'. This name was given him in jest, once again on account of his clothes, because he now wore a scarlet military jacket over a white kanzu. This jacket may have been the one issued to him when he served in Lugard's small police patrol in 1891. However, Dr Schofield[4] suggests it was a guardsman's red dress tunic, which had been given him by an English officer, probably Major Roddy Owen. Mrs Ruth Fisher confirmed this and tells how he would never be parted from it. One day he stood before her small looking-glass and patted his stomach, saying, '*Nyina kitinisa kingi, omuserikali wa Jesu*' ('I have great glory, a soldier of Jesus'). She also tells that when he was to be ordained a deacon in 1900 it was with great difficulty that he was persuaded to take off his favourite red jacket! Thus it won for him the name he was always to keep, and as he first went with the good news in his heart to Toro, he looked upon himself as 'the messenger of the good tidings from England'.

How different from his previous journeys along this road, a road he himself had once helped to clear. Now his burden was perhaps a box of gospels and the psalms in Luganda, his sleeping-mat and a few worldly possessions.

'There in Toro at the capital (the Mukama's capital at Kabarole was a short distance from Fort Gerry) I started work preaching the things of God. God was very kind to me in all my work for Him . . . I found fifty readers . . . and they were building a small church thirty feet long . . . so I found great joy from preaching and teaching the Gospel . . . it was quite different from anything else.'

This happy state of affairs was soon disrupted. In November an incident occurred which set the whole place in a ferment. As we have seen, the recent history of Toro had been one of invasion and confusion, and the condition of the country had not been improved by the introduction of the Sudanese, who looted whenever they could without scruple. At the same time the people were by no means all eager to acknowledge the authority of the young Mukama Kasagama, who, naturally enough, followed the familiar pattern of chiefly conduct in Africa of those times. In order to establish his newly acquired supremacy he sent punitive expeditions to subjugate dissident chiefs and to enrich himself with the quantities of women, slaves, guns, cattle, and ivory necessary to create his own chiefly prestige, quite disregarding the fact that he had signed two agreements promising to obey the British who had restored him, and to prevent slave raiding and arms trading in his country.[5] However, it is hardly likely that he understood the significance of these promises and his conduct led to considerable friction between himself and the British administrative officers in charge of Toro.[6]

Early in 1895 Kasagama raided a neighbouring Munyoro chief

called Rwaburdongo, capturing women, guns and other property, which he later refused to surrender on the orders of the British Government; consequently the newly arrived British officer in Toro, Captain Cromer Ashburnham, handled the situation in a very high-handed manner and arrested the Mukama, putting him in chains until the goods were produced. At the same time he ordered the Sudanese soldiers from the garrison to raid Kasagama's *kikale* or royal enclosure, where they found the chiefs and people hiding the property in the long grass. On recovery of the property Kasagama was released.

On 10 November of that year, when Ashburnham returned from a trip to Katwe to find that Kasagama had been entertaining a powder-running caravan from Uhaya, he again took drastic action. The traders were alleged to be staying in the nearby enclosure of the chief Nyakusuru, so Ashburnham led a surprise raid on this place that same night, only to find the caravan had decamped to a safe distance. Prisoners were taken to give evidence and the chief Nyakusuru was sent with a Sudanese patrol to lead them to where the powder had been buried. This was never found; the Sudanese no doubt handled their prisoner harshly and it was alleged that Nyakusuru was beaten so severely that he died the following day.

Kasagama fled as soon as he heard what was happening and quickly distributed his property, some of which was placed in the Christian teachers' house, situated close to the *kikale*. On hearing of Kasagama's flight the Sudanese raided the *kikale*, where nine powder kegs were found. There were also holes in the floor of Kasagama's hut where other kegs had been buried. At the same time the surrounding settlement was raided, including the houses of the teachers; the people fled, the teachers and their flock with them, 'and our books fell into the Mpanga river . . . the Englishman, Capt. Basibanamu (Ashburnham) arrested me (Apolo) with the teachers and fellow workers . . . and he took us into the fort at Toro'.

It appears that the teachers had claimed compensation for property said to have been stolen by the Sudanese previous to this last fracas. No doubt the mutual hatred between the people and the Sudanese led to endless complaints, trying the overstrained patience of the British officer; and when Apolo complained of further looting on this occasion of his own property and 4,000 cowrie shells belonging to the C.M.S.[7] Ashburnham accused him of lying and trying to blackmail the Administration. He also suspected the influence of the teachers with the Mukama, so Apolo and the other teachers were promptly sent off to Kampala along with the other prisoners.

Apolo was first shown the holes in the Mukama's floor, so that he could be used as a witness. He was then chained to the others and they were marched away to Kampala, carrying loads of ivory and boxes on their heads.[8] 'When I and my companions arrived at Kampala, they were released, but me they put in chains. I saw great sorrow in those chains—very great sorrow—but by the mercy of God I was released without trial . . . because when they took councel they saw there was no reason for me to be tied up. The soldiers had beaten me without a cause. They had done more to me than those with me, because I was the senior.'

Kasagama had taken refuge in the mountains, but was advised by the C.M.S. to come to Kampala to plead his case, which he did in January, before the Commissioner, Bishop Tucker and Archdeacon Walker. Ashburnham was called in to make his charges, the three main ones being slavery, illicit running of gunpowder, and bribing the Government interpreter.

Bishop Tucker's brief account of Kasagama's complete exoneration somewhat screens the whole business.[9] There is little doubt that Kasagama's dealings had been unlawful, but that Ashburnham's harsh and unwise handling of the situation made him also an offender. These unhappy incidents show up a situation that was far too difficult for an irascible young Army officer, who was at the same time ignorant of the language and at the mercy of an unscrupulous interpreter. Above all, he was unskilled in the art of handling an inexperienced young African chief, whose background could hardly help him to appreciate the new laws imposed upon him and his obligation to the protecting power. The situation was further bedevilled by religious rivalry. The Roman Catholic White Fathers had now established themselves near Kabarole and considerable bitterness arose between chiefs of different affiliations.

'Our pleasure', writes the Bishop, 'at the acquittal of the King and the vindication of the action of our teachers was naturally very great . . . Apolo Kivebulaya, who had been sent as a prisoner to Mengo, was released and compensation given him.' It was very important for the C.M.S. to secure a Protestant ruler in Toro. The Roman Catholics were already trying to convert Kasagama's mother, the Nyina Mukama.

Kasagama, who had been attending classes for religious instruction since his arrival in Kampala, was baptized by the Rev. E. Millar on 15 March 1896 in the presence of the Commissioner, and took the name of Daudi (David). He shortly returned to his own country, but not before extracting a promise from the Bishop to give him an English missionary.

'30 March 1896, we returned to Toro following Mr (A. B.) Fisher (the new missionary) and the Bishop.' The two hundred miles of tramping through elephant-grass, jungle, and swamp, wet through from tropical storms or steamy heat, were a feature of those times. The missionaries were accompanied by a string of porters carrying the necessary goods upon their heads and a day's march seldom covered more than about twelve miles. As they neared Toro the country gradually rose to a high plateau of tumbled hills spilt about the great purple bulk of the Ruwenzori mountains.

Fisher records: 'At last we reached the foot of the King's hill to find him seated on his leopard-skin mats on his chair of state surrounded by his mother and sister and all his chiefs. The great ones came forward first and greeted us in the Uganda fashion, by embracing us over the right and left shoulder in turn and wringing our hands, calling out many words of greeting and thanks. After the first formal greetings were over, we all moved off to the church, where a short service was held.'[10]

'Our first work was to call together the teachers and to consult with them as to the evangelization of the country. Seven districts were mapped out, and two evangelists sent to each. Then the examination of candidates for baptism was taken in hand and on Friday 8 May it was my joy to administer the holy rite to fifteen adults—eight men and seven women.'[11] Among the latter was the Nyina Mukama, who took the name of Vikitoliya (Victoria). The following day the Christian marriage of Daudi Kasagama was solemnized. The ceremony was followed by a great feast.

On 9 May Apolo records: 'They sent me to Nyagwaki in Busongora.' Southern Toro encompassed the eastern flank of Ruwenzori, whose towering presence dominates all who pass that way to the salt lake of Katwe, where for generations men have come to gather this precious commodity from its claret-coloured waters. So it was upon this ancient trail Apolo turned southwards, crossing the turbulent glacier-fed streams, until his path went up into the foothills where the Bakonjo villages clung to the almost vertical sides of the mountain. These sturdy people had for centuries been robbed and raided by the people of Toro and Bunyoro. They now cultivated the steep mountain slopes and hunted in the high-altitude forests.[12] The Bakonjo had harboured the fugitive Nyina Mukama and the young Kasagama on their flight towards Ankole when Kabarega's armies first invaded Toro, consequently Vikitoliya asked for Christian teachers to be sent to the Bakonjo: 'they are kind people, they did not betray me'.[13] Apolo may have had a Mutoro interpreter with him, as Lunyoro was very generally understood by most of the tribes of these regions. He himself could hardly have mastered the language, although Lunyoro-speaking people are able to understand Luganda reasonably well.

The response of these shy people to Apolo's teaching was slow. 'I was not very happy, because no one came to "read" for baptism, but they came to listen to the Gospel. I was pleased about that.' In September Fisher paid a visit to this isolated spot and tells of a small church built high in the foothills, where Apolo Kivebulaya met him with eight 'readers', and many of the mountain folk were learning; also the old people came just to listen to such *ebigambo ebirungi*—beautiful words.

Into the Congo

While Apolo was at Nyagwaki the Toro mission was concerned about its farthest outpost at Mboga, on the western side of the great Albert Rift Valley in what is now the Congo. At that time this territory west of the Semliki river was included within the British 'sphere of influence', the boundary between Belgian and British territory being marked by the supposed position of the 30 meridian of longitude east of Greenwich. The people of Mboga (Banyamboga) were originally pastoral Bahuma,[14] who had migrated across the Rift Valley from Mwenge Province, which was part of Bunyoro, possibly in the latter half of the seventeenth century. In 1896 the ruling Mukama Tabaro was the seventeenth encumbent of this sub-dynasty, established originally, it is said, by a chief called Isingoma of the *Muboro* clan, who got into trouble with the royal house of Bunyoro and fled to the high grassland west of the Semliki river, where he established the present dynasty and dominated the neighbouring tribes. The news of good grazing on the open grasslands bordering the great Congo forest led to three more early migrations from southern Bunyoro. It is told that Isingoma forbade intermarriage with the neighbouring tribes, and to this day the Banyamboga have retained their language and customs, while other migrations of Banyoro to the west of Lake Albert intermarried freely with the Balega and rapidly lost their language and social customs, although they retain their physical characteristics, religion, and cattle ritual.

The young Mukama Tabaro of Mboga succeeded his brother, who died in 1892. In recent times Kabarega's armies had held sway over all this territory until Lugard arrived at the Chief Kavalli's headquarters in 1891 to enlist the Sudanese garrison left there by Emin Pasha. In 1894 Tabaro crossed the Semliki to visit the newly installed Kasagama and asked that his territory might also come under British protection. There he heard about this new 'reading'. 'Kasagama told him it was good, as everyone in Buganda was reading.'

Tabaro therefore asked for Baganda teachers, and two of them,

Petero and Sedulaka, shortly followed him to Mboga, where they proceeded to build a small church near the *kikale*. But things did not go well. According to Yakobo Tebinderana, these Baganda found great difficulty in teaching the people; they were perhaps somewhat arrogant, and also refused to join in beer-parties, which were a constant feature of the Mukama's establishment. (It must be understood that from earliest times the Protestant Church in Uganda turned its face against beer-drinking because drunkenness was almost universal. Owing to the ease with which beer could be brewed from plantains, even the poorest could indulge in it; but it so obviously led to moral laxity and mental dullness.) As a result Tabaro forbade the people to feed the teachers who, being proud Baganda, would not cultivate for themselves (the work of women and slaves). They were therefore compelled to return to Toro.

In August 1896 Fisher and A. B. Lloyd (the latter had joined the Toro mission in July) visited Mboga, where they found the people enthusiastic for further teaching, but the Mukama not very keen. Fisher wrote, 'We were very anxious to place there a reliable teacher, and one of our very best, Apolo Kivebulaya volunteered to go and was joined by another Muganda, Sedulaka.'

Later in the year, therefore, Apolo was recalled from Nyagwaki and asked to take over the work at Mboga. He tells how he climbed the northern spur of Ruwenzori behind Kabarole. 'There I stood and looked far away to the Congo. The prospect terrified me. Then in December 1896 I went there to preach in that country.'

The immensity of the scene from the 8,000-foot ridge where Apolo stood is overwhelming: 6,000 feet below the floor of the Rift Valley is a bush-dotted plain flecked with sun and cloud shadow; here and there a silvery gleam shows the Semliki river winding its sinuous way to join the shimmering expanse of Lake Albert to the north; beyond this the Balega hills rise steeply into the misty haze and westwards the dark Congo forest fades into infinite distance. In this remote watershed of the Nile the excess of nature's wealth is in contrast to the sparseness of the human population, the remnants of ancient peoples, and of other more recent arrivals, but all reduced to a form of human stagnation.

It was into this darkness that these two brave-hearted teachers, Apolo and Sedulaka, set out with their boxes of reading sheets and gospels. Perhaps a number of porters carrying food accompanied them as they left the shelter of the mission at Kabarole and followed the winding path past the Nyina Mukama's gardens to the edge of the Toro plateau, where the high country plunges 3,000 feet to the plains below, now shimmering in the heat haze and smoke of innumerable grass fires of the dry season (December). The precipitous path, scoured into deep runnels by flood water, brought them down into the intense heat of this low country, uninhabited by man and teeming with great herds of game. It is said that Apolo never armed himself on these journeys; however, wild animals seldom molest man unless he disturbs them. At night they may have slept in a hunter's hut or built themselves shelters of branches and grass; a substantial fire kept burning all night would keep marauding animals away. A two-day march would bring them to the banks of the Semliki, where a few hunters and fishermen had their huts; here they would stay the night and hire a dug-out canoe to take them across the fast-flowing Semliki the following day. Another day would bring them to the foothills of the western wall of the Rift. Here there were open grass-covered hills with tree-lined streams and patches of cultivation in the valleys.

The story of Apolo's first coming to Mboga is told by Ibrahimu Katalibara. 'After Apolo crossed the Semliki he stayed at the hut of Mwemi, who asked him what he was going to do at Mboga. "I am a *nyakatagara* (diviner)," said Apolo. "Good," said Mwemi, "for I am *nyakatagara* to the Mukama Tabaro." Apolo answered him, "I also go to prophesy and I will prophesy for you in the morning." "That's good," said Mwemi, and cooked food for him—a true sign of fellowship.

'When the day broke, Apolo said, "I want to get off early, but I'll show you my divining before I go." He opened the Gospel of St John and read "For God so loved the world that He gave His only begotten Son, that whosoever believeth in Him should not perish, but have everlasting life", and explained to him Jesus, that

"Who so believeth shall be saved". But it seems that the diviner was not impressed.

'As Apolo passed through patches of forest on his journey he cut some hoe handles; he knew that the teachers before him had been forced to leave because of hunger.' Before long, the cluster of grass huts forming the Mukama's enclosure came into view, nestling against a high ridge and surrounded by millet gardens.

Ibrahimu continues: 'When Tabaro saw Apolo with his hoe handles he said, "Here comes a man who is going to conquer." When he had greeted Tabaro, Apolo explained his need for a garden. He had truly come to be a teacher, but he wanted to "get the garden dug". Tabaro beat the drum and called the people together. They all helped him; among the crowd was the Nyina Mukama (Mother of Tabaro) who clapped her hands and said, "We have got an undefeatable Muganda." They at once felt his personality and brought him food. "We will feed you until your garden produces." '

Tabaro assigned three young lads in their teens from his own family to the teachers' household, to work for them and learn at the same time. They were Yakobo Tebinderana, Daudi Ndagamberaha, and Petero Kamihanda. All three were baptized in April 1897. They helped to build the teachers' house, which was square with openwork reed walls and a thatched roof, unlike the local round grass huts.

However, there was no warm response to Christian teaching, partly because the first teachers had been so easily driven away. Apolo records, 'I did not remain well, because when I got there I did not see any good, their faith was weak, but I found one woman, Elizabete Ruhubya (he gives her the name she later took at baptism), who wanted very much to trust our Lord Jesus. She came to me and said, "I want you to write me down to read for baptism." I said to her, "Go and call your husband." He came, with spear and throwing stick, and said to me, "If you baptize my wife I will spear you." I said, "I shall not baptize her, the Englishman will, I shall just write her name down and she will come to be instructed." He then went to see the Mukama, who was related to him; and said, "It is you who brought this reading, go and be baptized with my wife, then I shall allow her to be baptized." After this, the

Mukama came to see me and said "Leave this woman alone, she is bad. I know her. I brought the reading here, let me read. You are an important person, this woman will do you no good." I replied, "Alright, although she is bad, let me write her name down, and I will see how bad she is for myself".'

A visit from the missionary, Lloyd, in January helped to get the matter settled and the Mukama agreed to allow people to read for baptism. 'There came twelve others to follow that woman, and her husband came to read, his name was Muchwangobe, they were both baptized, the husband by the name of Zakaliya and his wife Elizabete.' Fourteen people were baptized at Mboga on 4 April 1897 by the Rev. J. S. Callis.[15] This first little group of baptized Christians were mostly young boys in their teens and two young girls, three or four older men, and two women—Elizabete Ruhubya and Damari Ngaju—the latter was one of the Mukama's numerous wives; these two women played a prominent part in the life of this embryo church. The Mukama now showed interest in the teaching and had himself and thirty followers written down for baptism. Apolo remarked, 'We were teaching the good things.'

Later in April, however, disaster swept down upon Mboga. A body of 2,000 Manyuema armed with guns had mutinied from the Belgian expedition led by Baron Dhanis against the Mahdists in the upper reaches of the Nile.[16] They were now moving southward with the intention of raiding the rich cattle people of Busongora in southern Toro. These ruthless people moved like a scourge across the country, burning and looting as they went. On 27 April Captain Claude Sitwell, now commanding at Fort Gerry, received a message from Apolo that these Manyuema had attacked Tabaro's and Baligyangera's villages, carrying off women, children, and property.[17] Apolo records, 'They burnt the church and set fire to the buildings around and looted; we were driven out into the long grass. Later on we all came back.

'After this one of the Mukama's children died, then the Mukama said, "There is no God; let them bring back the charms and incantations." Twenty people from the *kikale* left the class; the ten who remained were driven out from the *kikale*.'

The Manyuema came raiding a second time, 'and we again fled for five days, taking refuge in the wild country of the Semliki plain.' Père Achte of the Roman Catholic White Fathers' Mission was at this time on his way across the Semliki plains on a missionary journey when he fell into the hands of the mutineers, who kept him prisoner for five days. 'I was very nearly killed . . . They robbed me of all; I have only my shirt left.'[18] However, he persuaded them against attacking Fort Gerry, where he knew Sitwell had only a small force of Sudanese, so they continued south and west of Ruwenzori to the abandoned Belgian post at Karimi. A party of the mutineers then attacked the small garrison at Katwe, who drove them off. Strife and smallpox within their own ranks further weakened them. One party submitted to the Belgians at Stanley Falls. Those who remained in the area were finally defeated by the Belgians.

Accused of murder

The priests and diviners attributed the recent misfortunes of Mboga to the presence of the teachers. In addition, the Mukama Tabaro began to resent the interest that some of the women in his *kikale* were taking in this new teaching; they were becoming independent, and insisting on going to read. He also imagined they would be taken to wife by the teachers, who were not of his tribe. These women were finally driven out of the *kikale*.

Yakobo relates: 'It is quite understandable that the visitors had been welcomed to his (Tabaro's) country, Apolo talked kindly to him about drunkenness and beating people, but now his influence was getting too strong and Tabaro began to try to get the Christians to drink beer and return to heathen practices.'

Not only were the women acting independently, but men like his relative Zakaliya stood their ground against the Mukama, who imagined that they were plotting to usurp his kingdom, for those who 'read' were popular with the British. Apolo lamented: 'He abused and slandered these people and commanded their books to be destroyed. Some of those who had believed on Jesus went back, for fear of the Mukama. He persecuted them constantly, and when these went back I was very troubled and asked myself, "Are all going to leave the class?", but the All-powerful God, He helped us and all the sheep were not scattered.'

Yakobo tells that 'Apolo was very courageous. Tabaro was by now eager to get rid of him; he feared his growing authority, and who was to know this might not be a political move from Buganda to get rid of the Mukama? For these reasons Tabaro refused the Christians a piece of ground for the rebuilding of the church, hoping always that Apolo would go away'.

Apolo listed briefly the Mukama's commands. '(i) You are not to build a church here. (ii) Christians may not visit others, anyone found visiting will be beaten. (iii) You are not to feed the teachers, let them die of hunger or drive them away.'

It is clear that Tabaro feared reprisals from the British if he openly murdered the Christian teachers. He was a weak and vacillating young man and the councils of the diviners and witch-doctors had great influence over him. As a gesture he left his *kikale* for a time and took up residence on a neighbouring hill.

The Christians held their ground, Elizabete feeding and caring for the teachers. 'Our eyes fell on a large tree and it was here that we met for prayers.'

Sedulaka, it seems, had gone back to Toro during this difficult time, to seek advice from the C.M.S. mission.[19]

In January 1898 Apolo tells how this tenacious little group decided to build their church, come what may. 'We went to see our friend Zakaliya Muchwangobe. We asked him for a spear to dig the holes for planting the posts and we left it propped up against the wall of our house while we went to mark out the site. Then we noticed a great fire burning (January is the dry, hot time of the year when the grass is like tinder; before a stiff breeze a fire will get completely out of control) behind the *kikale*, we were near the entrance. It was coming near our house and we went to put it out, but it was too fierce, so we tried to get the things out of the house, we were in a line, running to help, whoever had put the spear down had not made it secure, for it was leaning at an angle, and Malyamu Tiguita (the Mukama's sister) fell on it and she died, January 20.'

Yakobo had been using the spear which had been borrowed from Yohana, son of Zakaliya and Elizabete. Yakobo said that when he came out of the house he saw Apolo bending over the girl, who said, 'This girl has fallen on your spear.' 'What shall we do?' asked Yakobo. Apolo answered, 'Go and tell the Mukama.' Frightened though he was, Yakobo turned to obey, and got as far as the gate of the *kikale*, where the Mukama could be seen drinking, and drums were playing. Yakobo was afraid to go and tell the Mukama, as he was bound to ask, 'To whom did the spear belong?' and he feared arrest.

When he got back to Apolo, Malyamu was dead. Although Yakobo was using the spear it really belonged to Yohana's father, so Yakobo said in panic, 'I am going to run away', and Yohana said, 'I am coming too, for the spear belonged to my father.' They ran off to Nakabale and hid in a cleft between the rocks.

The death wailing had begun, and on enquiring who was dead the Mukama was told that Malyamu had been killed by Yakobo, and that he and Yohana had fled. He at once sent men to search for them. However, it was then suggested by the elders that Apolo had killed her, so a somewhat drunken rabble converged on the teacher's house. Apolo records, 'I saw much sorrow that day. They came with spears and sticks and surrounded my house, and I was inside it. They stuck the spears through the walls, as a fisherman would spear fish in a basket trap. They were afraid to come into the house, in case I had a spear, but I had none. Then I started to pray. When they could not break through they left off.

'Then a man called Balega, a nephew of the Mukama, said, "Let us bring fire and burn him out." He ran to fetch embers, he visited six houses before he found any, all this running about took half an hour. When at last he brought the fire, God my Father, having power over all things raised up a woman, the Mukama's mother, who shouted in a loud voice "If you kill that man Apolo, who is alone in his house, without a reason, you will be killed. If you kill that man Apolo, people will think you killed Malyamu because previously you persecuted the teachers." It was perhaps for this reason that God had prepared this woman, for Kayafa the chief diviner thought that he could rid the earth of me and was in league with this woman, who wanted her son to triumph and not really to save me (they feared the British might depose Tabaro), but it was that which my God had prepared to save me.'

Some of the Christians standing near were beaten, including Elizabete; subsequently some of them fled to Toro. It is told that Apolo finally came out of his house clasping an axe; Yakobo was told this; he, of course, was not present. Apolo said, 'If anyone comes near I will fell him', but the Nyina Mukama assured him he would not be killed, so he put the axe down. No doubt he was very afraid, surrounded by a group of people much the worse for drink, lusting for blood and excitement.

The Mukama said, 'You must not bring this girl's body into the *kikale* (for fear of her spirit), bring Apolo's bark-cloth and blanket and we will bury her in them', and she was buried at the door of Apolo's house. The house was then burnt to the ground.

'Then the Mukama took council to send me to the chief Baligyangera at Mitego, to whom the girl had been promised in marriage, that he might kill me.' Apolo was bound and sent off with an escort who beat him with the shafts of their spears. It is also told that at Mitego they tied him to a tree and beat him.[20] However, Baligyangera did not care to have this man's blood on his hands and sent him under escort to the British officer at Toro to answer a charge of murder, along with an elephant's tusk; something in the nature of a fee, perhaps.

The vision at Fort Gerry

When Apolo arrived at Fort Gerry he was put in prison. It was possibly then, in his dark hour of need, that he had a great spiritual experience. 'Jesus Christ appeared to me in a dream in the night when I was doubting if I could endure being bound and prodded with spears, and my house being burnt, being beaten every day and reviled and looked at with evil eyes. These were the things that were trying to drive me from the Congo. When I was thinking about these things I saw Jesus Christ shining like the sun, and He said to me: "Be of good cheer, I am with you." I answered and said:

"Who is speaking to me?" He replied the second time saying "I am Jesus Christ. Preach to my people. Do not be afraid." These were the things of my dream and they are quite true. Since that year until now when I preached to the people they turned quickly from their customs and repented.'[21]

It is not possible to say just when Apolo had this dream; he did not record it until many years later, but it is clear that it was connected in his mind with the persecutions he had suffered, and from then on there followed a great deepening of his spiritual life. In his diary he wrote, 'From that time I was utterly certain that I could not deny God, one little bit, and I was overcome with shame when I remembered the many times He had been merciful to me: therefore it is very difficult for me to leave Him. I am very much in awe of Him, because He is my helper. My spirit is very happy and I walk joyously, for I understand that God helps me more than anybody on earth—Is it not written "The Lord is my helper, I will not fear" (Heb. 13.6). If He should leave me, who will help me? He does not leave one ever; I am very happy and go about with great joy in my heart. Jesus Christ protects me and He has said "I will never leave thee" (Heb. 13.5). When I read that I was filled with great joy.'

The joy that came to Apolo then never seems to have left him; a joyous spirit was one of his most characteristic qualities, and his claim to being able to influence people through his preaching was certainly no idle one. He had a great understanding of people and a real gift for making them understand the truths he taught.

Apolo remained in prison to await his trial, as Sitwell had been ordered away with his Sudanese troops to intercept Mwanga,[22] who had again rebelled, and was trying to join the fugitive Kabarega north of the Nile. The Rev. T. R. Buckley of the C.M.S. was in charge of the Government station during Sitwell's absence and kept a kindly eye on Apolo. He recorded that 'when Apolo was in prison awaiting his trial he was still the Ambassador for Christ. He asked me to let him have some paper so that he might teach his jailers to write, that he might gain some influence with them and so gradually get them to take an interest in the teachings of Christ'.[23]

'When the Englishman came back, Mr Buckley told him everything and he stood up for me. He then told Buckley, "Take charge of him and bring him back when his accusers arrive."

'The Lord Jesus gave me very great strength, so that I was not discouraged in the work of our God. God has great mercy on those who trust Him. I trusted Him and He caused me to overcome. He hears the prayers of those who trust Him, as our Luganda proverb says *Engali alwade nabambula gwobuza edagala*? (Do you not seek advice from those who have been through the same thing?) They had taken me and released me from my chains, I prayed to God and He helped me very much, my enemies did not defeat me, even a little bit. This I understood, the many things which I have prayed for were not lost. God has answered my prayers (I have seen them). I had been very troubled where I was sent to teach and said to myself "Perhaps they will not believe in Jesus Christ", but whenever I prayed to the Lord they believed; when I did not continue in prayer they went back.'

Back to Mboga

Meanwhile at Mboga the two boys Yakobo and Yohana remained in hiding, fed by Elizabete. The Mukama's jealous cousin Sulemani Karemesa (a convert to the Roman Church, which was already at work in the Mboga area) saw here an opportunity to get the Mukama into trouble by accusing him to the British of the murder of the missing boys, and the place was in an uproar. 'To save the land from bloodshed Zakaliya revealed that the boys were alive.' Tabaro, greatly relieved to have the boys, took them to Toro with two of his chiefs to settle the dispute.

The case was heard by the Government officer and Tabaro was fined a quantity of ivory to make up losses of property sustained by Apolo and the C.M.S.

Then the Mukama asked that the teachers should return with him. Apolo and Sedulaka readily agreed to go back. Their desire for evangelism had been tested and they had not been found wanting. Apolo's diary gives the date of their return to Mboga as 24 April, but it was probably early June.[24]

'We set out together to go to Mboga, and when we got back we remained friends. The Mukama was converted and baptized and he remained faithful to the religion. This was done through our God, for many people thought it impossible that the Mukama should begin to "read" again. We did not return to sorrow; I remember the words of Scripture "I am poor and needy, who will save me? Only the Lord" (Ps. 40.17). The Lord saved me, and we understood that God saves without spears or guns. It is I, Apolo Kivebulaya, and Sedulaka, and these are the things which caused us to understand the kindness of God.' Ibrahimu Katalibara relates how Apolo boldly asked Tabaro for the sacred drum Rusama to be used in church for calling the people to services. When Tabaro agreed to this 'the heathen were very, very surprised, and it was a great victory for the Gospel and for Apolo'. This drum was a symbol to the people of the tribal spirit; it was kept in a sacred enclosure and cared for by a woman guardian, it was revered and worshipped like a god, with its own shrine, offerings and priest, and it was carried before the Mukama on ceremonial occasions, but once it was used for other purposes it lost its power. He also relates how 'before baptism people brought their charms to be destroyed'.

In July, Apolo and Sedulaka came over to Kabarole in Toro for the Bishop's visit, and were to escort him to Mboga three weeks later. Bishop Tucker describes the welcome he and Dr Albert Cook received as they approached Kabarole. 'Our friends at Kabarole . . . inundated us with letters of warm welcome, as we journeyed on our way thither. Hill after hill we found crested with little groups of friends who had come out to welcome us. Here, as we came to a patch of long grass, there burst forth upon us Apolo Kivebulaya, with lots of young men and lads, all brimming over with joy and excitement. There, marching in regular order, was another detachment of young men, with Sedulaka and Asa Nkangali at their head . . . Then on again till the groups of friends became so numerous that our progress was greatly hindered. Eventually, however, we reached the Mission hill, on which great crowds were assembled, and where Kasagama and the Queen Mother welcomed us with many expressions of joy at our coming.'[25]

These great displays of welcome to visitors and newcomers were a feature of the early days in the Toro Church. After a strenuous safari to Katwe the Bishop and Dr Cook then set out for Mboga, escorted by Sedulaka. Apolo had seemingly gone on ahead to see that all was in readiness.

The Bishop wrote: 'Two days later we drew near to Mboga, our destination. Since leaving the Semliki we had been constantly ascending, and were now at a considerable elevation above the plain. Sedulaka, one of our teachers from Mboga, was leading the way and in answer to my oft-repeated question "Are we near?" he would only respond *Tunatuka* (we shall arrive). At length, while resting and enjoying the refreshment of a cup of tea, we had a remarkable proof of the fact that we were not far away from our destination; in a moment of quiet meditation there burst upon us, with a great shout, a crowd of young men and boys, at the head of whom was Apolo Kivebulaya, with cries of welcome repeated again and again, they surrounded us, and almost knocked us over in their eagerness to get a shake of the hand, and to tell their joy at our coming.

'We packed up our traps and started once more, and in less than half an hour met Tabaro himself and a great crowd of followers. Their welcome was no less warm than that of Apolo and his young men, but it was less demonstrative. On reaching Mboga itself the enthusiasm of the people knew no bounds. They came in upon us in great crowds, embracing and shaking hands with us again and again, and thanking us for coming to them. It was most touching to see their simple trust in us, and the fixed conviction in their minds that we were in some way to be a means of blessing to them . . .

'Shortly after our arrival, Buckley commenced the work of examining the candidates for Baptism and Confirmation. On Wednesday, 24 August, thirteen of the former, among whom was Tabaro the chief were baptized,[26] and seven of the latter received the laying on of hands. It was a day of great joy . . .

'Among those under instruction we found two Pygmies of the forest . . . It seemed quite clear to us that in the not distant future it might be possible to evangelize the Pygmy tribes from Mboga as a base.'[27]

NOTES

¹ Quotations from Apolo's diary are from now on more obvious; they will no longer be noted unless it appears necessary.

² 'A teacher of the Gospel', which also included teaching people to read the written word. In this sense only is the word 'teacher' used in this biography.

³ Ham Mukasa wrote a short and illuminating account of his life published in *The Wonderful Story of Uganda* by J. D. Mullins (C.M.S., 1st ed., 1904). He died in 1956.

⁴ All people contributing to the narrative in Part II, unless otherwise noted, are referred to in Appendix C.

⁵ Treaty with Kasagama, 14 August 1891: Captain F. D. Lugard, *The Rise of Our East African Empire* (1893), vol. ii, p. 188. Treaty made near Fort Gerry in Toro, Central Africa, 3 March 1894. Entebbe MSS. Inward 1894.

⁶ The following incidents are based upon the correspondence between Captain Cromer Ashburnham, the British officer stationed in Toro from August 1895 until May 1896, and Her Majesty's Commissioner at Kampala. These letters are in the Uganda Government Archives at Entebbe.

⁷ Cowrie shells were first brought into Uganda by the Arabs as a form of currency. They were threaded on fibre strips of 100. Their value fluctuated considerably. To begin with 200 cowries = 1 rupee, but at the turn of the century their value had fallen to 1,000 or 1,200 to the rupee. 'Thus the value of a £5 note was 75,000 shells. As 10,000 shells (called a *mutwalo*) was a full load for a man, it required 7½ men to convey the value of £5! The importation of cowries was prohibited in July 1901, but their use continued until 1905.' Sir Albert R. Cook, 'Further Memories of Uganda', *Uganda Journal*, vol. 2 (1934), p. 111.

⁸ The Rev. Yosia Kamuhigi remembers seeing Apolo in the chain gang on this occasion. The Arabs had first employed this mode of keeping prisoners, whereby each man wore a stout iron ring round his neck; this was connected by a length of chain to the neck ring of the next man. Speke's companion J. A. Grant mentions chain gangs of slaves in 1861, 'Never is the chain unfastened, day or night. Should one of a number require to move, the whole must accompany him.' J. A. Grant, *A Walk Across Africa* (1864), p. 72.

⁹ A. R. Tucker, *Eighteen Years in Uganda* (1908), vol. ii, pp. 39–41.

¹⁰ A. B. Fisher's diary, C.M.S. Archives.

¹¹ Tucker, *op. cit.*, vol. ii, p. 51.

¹² The Bakonjo are a Bantu tribe who speak a very archaic form of the Bantu language and may have been the precursors of the nearly allied Bantu elements of the Baganda and Banyoro. Sir H. Johnston, *The Uganda Protectorate* (1902), vol. ii, pp. 575–7.

[13] Fisher's diary.

[14] The people of Bunyoro and Toro are composed of two distinct races. The cattle-owning ruling class or Bahuma of Nilotic origin, and the Bantu cultivators or Bairu, who probably came from the west at a very much earlier date.

[15] Callis was a young missionary who had arrived from England nine months previously. He died at Butiti on 24 April 1897, having probably contracted tick fever on his visit to Mboga. In those days the disease was unknown and its symptoms attributed to sunstroke.

[16] 'They pretend to number 4,000, but I should put them down at 2,000.' Père Auguste Achte to Captain C. Sitwell. Katiemba 27 April 1897, Entebbe Archives, A4/8/1897. Sir John Gray, in *Uganda Journal*, vol. 17 (1953), pp. 18–20.

[17] Sitwell's correspondence on the Manyuema raids. Toro, 27 April 1897, Entebbe Archives, A4/8/1897, No. 261.

[18] Père Achte to Captain Sitwell, Katiemba, 27 April 1897.

[19] T. R. Buckley, 'Some Experiences in Uganda', *Uganda Church Review*, March 1933, p. 31.

[20] A missionary doctor who had once examined Apolo told me that he bore considerable scars upon his back due to being beaten. He was first beaten by the Sudanese soldiers in 1895 when in the chain gang. A hippo hide whip was usually employed for chastising prisoners.

[21] 'A Fragment from Apolo', *Uganda Church Review*, July 1931, pp. 89–90. Translated by the Rev. W. S. R. Russell. Both in his diary and in this letter he states that he had this dream in 1899, but it is evident from his diaries that he was at times very hazy about dates.

[22] Mwanga, chafing against the restrictions imposed upon him by the British Government, had secretly escaped and made his way to Buddu, where he rallied a force to make a stand against the British. A force of Sudanese under Major Trevor Ternan defeated Mwanga, who was given asylum by the Germans near Bukoba, and his infant son, Daudi Chwa, was proclaimed Kabaka of Buganda in his stead. In 1898 Mwanga escaped from the Germans and made his way to join Kabarega north of the Nile. In April 1899 both were captured and deported to the Seychelles.

[23] Buckley, *op. cit.*, p. 32.

[24] Sitwell only returned to Fort Gerry on 13 May 1898. There is also the following entry in his diary of 4 June: 'Tried cases—some chiefs from west of Semliki came in.'

[25] Tucker, *op. cit.*, vol. ii, p. 127.

[26] Tabaro took the name Paulo because, like Saul, he had persecuted the Christians.

[27] Tucker, *op. cit.*, vol. ii, pp. 138–43.

7

THE GROWING CHURCH IN TORO

Peace comes to Toro

A POLO was recalled to Toro in August 1899, as trouble had once again overtaken Mboga. The Belgians were contesting the right of the British to administer territory west of the Semliki river, and Belgian government officers were already exacting tribute from the chiefs in the Mboga area. Their methods were harsh, as the Rev. T. B. Johnson remarked. 'The main duty laid upon a government officer was to secure so much revenue, and his reputation for ability depended upon his success in getting it brought in, therefore there could be little scope for good for the individual administrator. Also the soldiers employed to enforce the tribute were drawn from the most savage and cannibal tribes; it was not surprising then that the treatment of the defenceless villagers was brutal.'[1] At Mboga the soldiers employed by the Belgians were kidnapping women and children and the situation was very unsettled.[2]

In these conditions the C.M.S. saw fit to withdraw its teachers from Mboga temporarily. The Mukama Paulo Tabaro accompanied Apolo and Sedulaka back to Toro, where he took up residence near Kabarole for some months until conditions at Mboga had settled down again. Ibrahimu Katalibara and Jamesi Diti were charged with the care of the little group of Christians left at Mboga. On his return Tabaro took with him a Muganda teacher called Samweri Rukoma. He arrived to find that Sulemani Karemesa had been made Mukama in his place by the Belgians.

Meanwhile Apolo had been sent to Kitagwenda in south-eastern Toro. Here he was troubled by the slowness of the people to understand the teaching. 'I worried because those who did understand were so few, yet I saw no wrong there, only good.' But it seems he was not there long; by the end of the year he was called to the centre at Kabarole to help H. E. Maddox, who had arrived some months previously, with translation work.

The C.M.S. mission here had been growing steadily, and in 1898 Tucker wrote of a 'well-ordered mission station' on Kabarole hill, and by the following year a dispensary and schoolrooms were in use. A wave of enthusiasm was now bringing many to 'read', which was a great delight to Apolo. 'At this time I was specially happy because the people at Kabarole believed and many were baptized—in those days I got fat in my spirit, because my nature is to get troubled in spirit when I see people are not coming to church. I cannot eat well, I just worry, and you who do this work, you know what it is.

'I worried, but the Lord gave me strength and power and I overcame. I understand that God the Father and the Son and the Holy Spirit are with me. I did not doubt at all that I was with God and He with me. I found it difficult to believe that God helped me until the Holy Spirit showed me, then I knew it was He who helped me. I had been very troubled, but the Lord heard me and saw my trouble and I never lacked anything, whenever I needed anything He gave it to me. *My great need is to have power to bring people to Jesus Christ and to have the life which He gives.* Now I have no more fear of Satan.

'I have such great joy that I do not feel the need of food, goats, cows, clothes, money, because the Lord is with me. I shall get these things without buying them, they come to me from the Lord. I try to do as it is written: "Seek ye first the Kingdom of God and all these things shall be added unto you" (Matt. 6.33). Remember this and you will receive.'

This encouraging situation at Kabarole was the direct result of the improved political condition of the country brought about in the latter part of 1899. Until then Kasagama's struggle to establish his power over his chaotic kingdom[3] was complicated for him by the prohibition of the traditional means to that end, coupled with the obedience required of him to the demands of the protecting power. British policy was still very tentative and the task of creating law and order depended much upon personalities.

Military officers with small garrisons of troops were the only body of men available to the Government until trained civil administrators could be sent to the country. Captain Sitwell was an able and gallant army officer, but on occasions impatient and irascible when dealing with the endless disputes of Kasagama and his chiefs. Owing to the past disruption of the country Kasagama's own authority was slight and many of the chiefs would not owe him allegiance. Religious rivalry between Protestant and Roman Catholic adherents did not improve matters. Kasagama, himself belonging to one faction (Protestant), did not take kindly to the stern impartiality of the British officer when rival claims and animosities flared up. Sitwell's difficulties must not be underestimated; intrigue and lying, government interpreters who were easily bribed, and his own lack of knowledge of the people and their language led to bewilderment and strain between himself and Kasagama, who threatened to give up his kingdom on two occasions in those early years. But fortunately the missionaries, who had a more sympathetic understanding, helped considerably to explain and soothe the indignation of both parties.[4] It must also be remembered that Sitwell's brave and decisive handling of the troops under his command, and their absolute loyalty to him during the Sudanese Mutiny towards the end of 1897, ensured the relative peace and security that had been so newly won for Toro.[5]

In 1899 the British Authorities had decided on a more definite policy for Toro. The Mukama was to have his council (*Rukurato*) of twelve principal chiefs modelled on the Buganda pattern.[6] Maddox tells how the *Rukurato* met every Monday, and the *Katikiro* was to be accessible always to try cases. The Mukama and his council were to be taught and assisted in governing the country by the British sub-commissioner Stephen Bagge,[7] whose consistent policy and patient guidance soon bore fruit. Maddox wrote in

December 1899: 'The result has been splendid. Kasagama is a new man, even his enemies admit it . . . Another great change has taken place, Baganda influence has decreased enormously, and in matters of state is now almost of no account. This is due to the definite policy of the British government and the desire of the king and people to maintain the integrity of their own kingdom'.[8]

Kasagama's supremacy was further established by the 1900 Agreement when Sir Harry Johnston, Her Majesty's Special Commissioner to Uganda, visited Toro to make a settlement of the land and territorial boundaries. Maddox translated the terms of the Agreement into Lunyoro and explained it to the Mukama and his chiefs. Fisher records, 'For some days the air was full of questions and answers, until the last word was said and the Agreement signed by the king and chiefs 26 June 1900'.

Sir Harry Johnston was a new kind of white man. He made endless enquiries about birds, beasts, and flowers. What was his object? Did he want to tax them? Why did he want to know the number? They were stimulated beyond measure.

One day Kasagama and his chiefs burst in upon Fisher in great excitement. Holding one hand on their mouths they called upon all their ancestors to help them. 'What now?' he asked. 'We are asked to catch specimens of all the animals and creatures in the country and bring them to him. How can we pay three rupees tax and then spend our time in the wilderness fighting animals?' 'The *Bulozi* wants you to capture baby elephants and he will remit your hunters 200 hut taxes for each baby elephant delivered to him, he wants to train them to work as they do in India and Burma. He does not want you to kill the tuskers, but to separate and capture the babies.' 'Well,' said the Mukama, 'what about the chimpanzees? My people are superstitious, they and our ancestors have always made blood-brotherhood and they never attack each other. They live in the tree tops, so how can we get them?'

Fisher went outside to the crowd of followers, chiefly clad in skins, all carrying spears, and said, 'The Batoro are a brave race, they are the masters in this country, they are not afraid of animals, no matter how big! You kill huge elephants for their tusks, which buy you cloth, now you say you cannot catch babies! Are you afraid to try?' In a moment the whole courtyard was full of men advancing and receding with poised spears, jumping into the air and calling out what they would do to enemies of all kinds. Thus fear and gloom were dispelled and they all went away to try. Meanwhile, the ordinary folk, especially the young people, kept the Commissioner's assistants busy collecting, fixing, drying and curing specimens.

The Commissioner had also brought a phonograph and persuaded Kasagama to speak into it. Fisher records, 'They all listened spellbound, then clapped their hands to their lips and bent down to the ground in fear and awe, then turning their hands up in the air shouted and danced with excitement calling out *Gagwa mahano! gagwa manhano!* (wonder falls) *Ai Bajungu bano!* (Oh these Europeans!). For days the Commissioner's courtyard was filled with men and women wanting to catch sight of the wonder box.

Fisher, who had returned to the Toro mission after two years pioneering a new mission station in Bunyoro, remarked on the improved conditions of the country. Slavery had disappeared (with the encouragement of the missionaries Kasagama had given freedom to all those slaves who desired it) and the mutilations so evident in the practice of witchcraft were much less conspicuous.[9] Roads were improved and rivers bridged, markets had increased and prices were fixed. A large Swahili trading village had grown up in Fort Portal. The undisciplined and pilfering Sudanese troops were well in hand and were better paid and encouraged to cultivate their own food. Better houses were being built on the square pattern and the people looked clean and happy. The stage was now set for progress.

It is worth noting here that during 1901 the British reasserted their authority over the area west of the Semliki, at least until the Boundary Commission had made its recommendations. They reinstated Tabaro as Mukama of the whole area, which remained under the supervision of the British Commissioner stationed at Fort Portal in Toro.

Response to Christianity

Since 1896 the Church had grown slowly with inevitable difficulties due to religious and political rivalry. John Callis remarked that 'in spite of these hindrances—or is it because of them?—the truth is rapidly spreading'.[10]

As yet the Christian converts came mainly from the households of Kasagama and his mother. The latter was almost as powerful a personage as her son. She had built a very nice church at her own enclosure at Ngoma, two miles from Kabarole. But the majority of chiefs whose allegiance to the Mukama was still uncertain showed little desire for conversion. The peasantry naturally followed the chief's choice of religion where the chief had any influence; but the general disunity, poverty, and backwardness often made mission work very disheartening. The missionaries deplored the general indolence, sexual promiscuity, and drunkenness of the people; physically they were not robust and many suffered from respiratory diseases. Fisher remarked that 'drunkenness is the curse of this country and perhaps kills more than half of the population in time, after attending drinking orgies at night they fall down dead drunk and lie in the cold until morning'.

Yet, on the other hand, there were also hidden potentialities in these people. The sincere desire of the Mukama for his country to become Christian, the susceptibility of the people to influence and the readiness of the young to be taught. How greatly did this young mission beg for more missionaries, both men and women, and for a medical missionary to itinerate widely and win the shy suspicious heathen, who would come readily for medicine. 'Healing of sickness is so much the most prominent idea in these people's notions of religion, that it is, humanly speaking unreasonable to expect them to give up what they believe to be efficacious (witchcraft) while offering them nothing in return . . . The people are undoubtedly in earnest, but their earnestness, unless encouraged by careful training, does not lead to much. It is no small thing that the King, *Katikiro* and several chiefs attend one class a day regularly and sometimes two.'[11]

In assessing the work already done Maddox said, 'The proportion of Christians who care anything for the Lord Himself out of the number of those who have received Christian baptism is small . . . The novice who compares expectation with reality will be deeply disappointed . . . The more experienced missionary who compares the former state of these people with their present, will have an overpowering sense of God's almighty power.'[12]

In 1900 Maddox and Apolo were working hard at translating St Matthew's Gospel into Lunyoro, also a short form of morning and evening prayers. In pleading the case for having the Scriptures in Lunyoro Maddox wrote, 'Apolo Kivebulaya, who, as you know, first translated St Matthew, knows more about the country and this question especially, than any other Muganda, and his testimony as to the ease with which the Gospel is understood in the vernacular is most positive. He has been here for six years and knows the language very fairly. It is quite safe to say that he is absolutely the most influential missionary among the people generally that Toro has ever had. Firstly, this is due to his intense earnestness in the things of God, and secondly, to his knowledge of the language and customs of the people . . . Apolo is so eager on this subject and has it so much to heart that I have asked him to write you a letter expressing his opinions.'[13]

In April 1900 the arrival of two English lady missionaries in answer to Kasagama's prayer in 1896, 'Give us women, women will learn from women, give us light', caused much excitement. The ladies, Miss Edith Pike and Miss Ruth Hurditch, described the way Apolo Kivebulaya had prepared for them as they were arriving at Kabarole. He warned them that all the women in the country were congregated just behind the next hill. 'We little guessed what an army lay there. There as we turned the corner one mass of fluttering white, crimson and orange saris came bearing down upon us, clapping their hands and shrieking. Crowds of brown arms were thrown around us and they hugged us over the right and left shoulders. Our progress was slow, as from time to time new arrivals greeted us in the same emotional fashion. After about five miles of this, the male population came out headed by the stately 6 feet 4 figure of the King Kasagama followed by his chiefs and hundreds of his people . . . The royal band came to play us in, with drums and horns, which lasted nearly all night . . .'[14]

Both ladies were immediately precipitated into teaching women and children and dispensary work, together with the difficult matter of learning the language. Their coming 'created great interest and brought much people together. This gave opportunities for meetings and for encouraging those Christians who had given up coming to church'.[15]

The ideal of a Christian womanhood was an overwhelming need, and had to be won in the face of tribal customs, polygamy, and the past degradation of women to the status of slaves and a means of barter. The peasant women of Toro were indolent and backward. Miss Hurditch, who later became Mrs Fisher, described the monotony of their existence. Outside their tasks of cultivating and cooking 'the generality of them desire nothing so much as to sit still and do absolutely nothing . . . huddled together in their dirty little grass homes, their conversation scarcely ever ventured outside the well-beaten track of real or imaginary sickness, and the most revolting topics that polygamy and heathenism suggest'.[16]

With the coming of the lady missionaries the women of the royal household led the way in cleanliness, child care, and industry; the missionaries remarked on the change of expression to be seen on the faces of heathen women who had grasped the truth of Christian teaching, and the order and cleanliness that gradually came to be seen in their homes and gardens.

A visit to Mboga

Apolo records his ordination on 21 December 1900. 'The Bishop of Uganda laid hands upon me and made me a servant in the Church, a deacon in the Church of Toro, Kabarole. Then we set out from Kabarole with Mr Maddox (to visit Mboga). We slept at Wasa and met together with the 20 porters. In the morning we went to the house of Bambyeba and tried to get people together for a service, without success. In the evening Mr Maddox went to hunt buck but failed to get any. We returned and had prayers with the porters.' Three days later they reached Mboga and found a congregation of 400 in the church on Sunday. They stayed there long enough for Apolo to baptize fifty people and perform eighteen Christian marriages.[17]

On the return journey from Mboga the missionary party travelled south-east towards Ruwenzori to visit the Baamba tribe, who cultivated the immensely fertile valleys among the western foothills of the mountain. These people were of ancient Bantu stock, and very unlike their neighbours the Bakonjo or the Batoro. They went naked except for a loincloth, and their mops of long hair were twisted into thin strands and streamed with locally prepared castor oil. Sharply filed teeth and lips pierced with iron rings gave them a wild and barbarous appearance. They built their round beehive huts, thatched with plantain leaves, on either side of a clearing in the forest, forming a street. The larger the family groups, the longer the street. A village always included a common club-house where the villagers collected to smoke and chat. Each village was a separate entity ruled over by an elder, whose authority extended only over the limits of the village and family. There were no superior chiefs to whom all owed allegiance, and dissension between villages was common. It is alleged that these people practised cannibalism[18] and were similar in origin and customs to the Bahuku tribe of the Congo forest in the area west of Mboga, which Apolo was to evangelize in later years.

As the missionary party approached the great wall of Ruwenzori and entered the dense forest of the foothills, they were sure to have stepped aside to marvel at the boiling springs, whose columns of steam could be seen many miles away; the saline waters bubbled out of small blowholes in which food could be cooked with great rapidity. Then they made their way to a nearby Baamba village.

'We got to the house of Tende at Bundu and about forty Baamba met together and we preached to them. This was the first time that an Englishman from the mission had passed through Bwamba, for me also, I was the first teacher to tell them about God. Next morning we went to the house of Bugali and met with fifty people there.

Next day we went on and slept at the house of Ruhandika and met with ten Bakonjo.'

This mention of Ruhandika shows that they had climbed a precipitous mountain track for 4,000 feet to where the Bakonjo inhabited the higher slopes of the mountain. Ruhandika was chief of the Bakonjo of this area. He was described as a fine, powerful man, living in a village perched high on a mountain ledge. His huts were well built and strengthened by bands of tough boughs encircling the thatch as a protection against the gales that swept the high ridges. His numerous wives were heavily decorated with iron ornaments and plaited grass rings on their necks, arms, and ankles.[19] A sturdy, hard-working people, the mountain Bakonjo were often employed as labourers on the land by the Batoro.

After leaving Ruhandika the party had a stiff climb of perhaps another 2,000 feet to the ridge of the northern spur of the mountain, where they could look down upon the Toro side. Perhaps through a gap in the forest they would see the craggy summits and glistening snowfields of the range to the south of them. Then 3,000 feet below lay Toro, its hills dwarfed like the waves of the sea, its crater lakes set like gems in the green, and Fort Portal with 'its houses and huts, its broad roads, its fort and its two churches laid out as on a map'.[20] The descent would be rapid, and as they skirted the Nyina Mukama's gardens perhaps a messenger would be sent in with compliments, and along the broad road the caravan would inform everybody of their arrival with a chorus of hearty yells.[21]

NOTES

[1] T. B. Johnson, *Tramps Round the Mountains of the Moon* (1912), p. 218.

[2] John Roscoe, Toro, Annual letter, 10 February 1899, C.M.S. Archives. See also Sir Harry Johnston, *The Uganda Protectorate* (1902), vol. i, pp. 197–8.

[3] 'Toro Proper' consisted of the country immediately east of the Ruwenzori Mountains and to some distance just north of the range. In 1894 Major Owen formed a confederacy of southern Bunyoro chieftaincies, who were ready to owe allegiance to Kasagama. This was known as the 'Toro

Confederacy'. *Enquiry into the Grievances of the Mukama and People of Toro* (Uganda Government Press, 1926).

[4] The information in this paragraph is based upon Captain C. H. Sitwell's 'Uganda Diary, 1895–99' in MS., in Secretariat Library, Entebbe; and the Rev. A. B. Fisher's diary, C.M.S. Archives.

[5] Sir John Gray, in *Uganda Journal*, vol. 17 (1953), pp. 22–23.

[6] Unlike Buganda, there did not exist the same formal political hierarchy among the different ranks of chiefs of the Lunyoro-speaking people.

[7] Sitwell left Toro in December 1898 and Stephen Bagge took up his duties there in March 1899.

[8] Maddox to Baylis, Toro, 4 December 1899, C.M.S. Archives.

[9] It was common to see babies and small children scarred with knife cuts and burns, inflicted upon them to drive out evil spirits.

[10] R. D. Pierpoint, *In Uganda for Christ* (Life of the Rev. J. S. Callis) (1898), p. 154.

[11] Maddox to the Secretary of C.M.S., Toro, 13 January 1900, C.M.S. Archives.

[12] Maddox to Baylis, Toro, April 1899, C.M.S. Archives.

[13] Maddox to the Secretary of C.M.S., Toro, 8 September 1900, C.M.S. Archives.

[14] Fisher's diary.

[15] Maddox, Annual letter, Toro, 4 December 1900, C.M.S. Archives.

[16] Ruth B. Fisher, *On the Borders of Pygmyland* (1905), pp. 70–71.

[17] A. B. Fisher, Kabarole, 25 February 1901, *Church Missionary Intelligencer* (1901), p. 627.

[18] E. H. Winter, *Bwamba* (1956), pp. 133–50.

[19] Johnson, *op. cit.*, pp. 180–1.

[20] Major R. E. Jack, *On the Congo Frontier* (1914), p. 107.

[21] Johnson, *op. cit.*, p. 182.

8

MISSIONARY JOURNEYS

────────

A year in Butiti

'1 MARCH 1901: They sent me to Butiti.' This is in the lovely
open cattle country of Mwenge district. Apolo was sent to
breathe new life into a Church that had waxed and waned considerably in the eight years of its life. Apolo tells how 'we were
troubled in spirit whether people would come to church, they
listened and agreed and lots of them came. It was like a person going
to wait for the ants to come out of the ant-hills. He sees an opening,
and he knows they are going to come out, he says "Perhaps the
wind will come and they won't come out." That man is anxious
without a cause, he is worried because he does not know what is
going on inside the ant-hill, because he cannot see—so we men do
not really know what is going on in God's purposes . . . but God
saw us and had great mercy on us, God called the people and they
came into the church'.

Some months later Maddox wrote that the result of Apolo's special
mission to Butiti had been instantaneous. Armed with Lunyoro
reading sheets, the catechism and perhaps St Matthew's gospel in
Lunyoro, he soon drew the people. 'Apolo is most emphatically a
man of prayer, and within a few days came little notes telling of
increased attendance in church, sales of books and great successes in
the outlying gardens.'[1] In August 1901 Fisher recorded: 'The congregation at Butiti has more than doubled under the able and energetic
pastor Apolo Kivebulaya . . . He induced hundreds to commence
reading and sold a very large quantity of Lunyoro literature.'[2]

That same year Apolo went on three missionary journeys into southern Toro, visiting and encouraging the teachers already at work in the churches and preaching Christ in new places, as well as performing baptisms and marriages. One was with Maddox to Muhokya. They crossed Lake George in a dug-out canoe, the missionary's cows attached by rope having to swim alongside; cows always accompanied these safaris to supply milk. They returned through Kitagwenda. One point of interest here was that Tito Balikurungi was now a teacher at Kitabu (Nyagwaki); he was one of the first group to be baptized at Mboga.

Later in the year Apolo escorted the lady missionaries on a journey to Lake George. Miss Hurditch remarked, 'Certainly we could not have had an escort more respected and beloved all round these parts than good old Apolo.'

They set forth in the rainy season. The ladies, wearing long Edwardian skirts, must have found the cycling and tramping through tall wet grass and mud very heavy going. However, when the sun shone 'we steamed along on our machines (solid-tyred bone-shakers!) with sun hats and big sun-shades, over ridges and through mud at which even a horse would stop and consider. Our noble Apolo insisted on keeping pace with our bicycles, and as small batches of natives passed on the road, gazing with blank astonishment at the "running snakes", he called out with pride and elation, "Look at the wisdom of the white man!".'[3]

At each village (generally a chief's or headman's residence surrounded by a cluster of retainers) they halted and in many received a great welcome. People flocked to see the first white women. If they were to stay the night, food would be brought for the caravan in exchange for reading sheets, hymn books or gospels—where the people were reading, or if not they paid with calico, cowrie shells or beads. At Butanuka they spent three days and 'were besieged with callers. The sick came in for medicine, readers to be questioned for baptism, and others desirous of being written down for instruction. A teacher from a neighbouring village was sent to us with an eager request that we should visit them . . . Although the teacher had only been there at work one month we found quite a lively interest had been awakened among the people. The chief of the village, who was a captain of the King's soldiers, came out in big style to welcome us. After a little service and a great deal of medicining, we were taken to the chief's hut, where a meal had been prepared for us. After seating ourselves on soft, fresh grass that had been laid upon the floor we started operations. First of all water was brought in for hand ablutions, then the unsweetened cooked bananas (*bitoke*) were brought in, and a boiled chicken, all wrapped up in the banana leaves in which they had been cooked. The chicken was broken up into tempting morsels by our host and an immoderate helping of bananas was plumped down in front of each (laid out on smoked banana leaves). Then commenced the process of rolling the bananas into small balls in our hands, and punching a depression in the middle by which the gravy could be scooped up. A sheep and three chickens were brought to us as presents, and as we started off, nearly the whole village followed behind. In spite of hurrying we did not reach home (camp) before darkness fell, and a thunderstorm broke over us, extinguishing the long, flaming torches which the natives carried, so we had to push along as best we could and arrived in a wearied and very bedraggled condition'.[4]

Apolo continues, 'The next night we slept at Buhwezi. About 35 met together, we found their faith weak. We went on to Kanyamuro to the house of Mutagwanda. We prayed by ourselves as the people refused to come. We went to Mubuku and gathered about 25 people; we preached to them of the love of Christ, and for those that believed on Him, how He gives them the things they need.'

At Muhokya they pitched their tent in the fishermen's village, reeking of drying fish, mingled with the odours of the huts, where cattle, sheep, chickens, and people all huddled together. The next day they climbed the spur of Ruwenzori to visit Apolo's old station at Nyagwaki (he now refers to this place as Kitabu) where streams of people came down the path to meet them and help push them up the steeper parts. 'About 100 were in church. We praised them for their perseverance, and their teacher for helping them forward. We spoke of the glory they would have in the world to come. In the afternoon I baptized four women. Miss Pike preached that they had now become soldiers of Christ and they would have a place in heaven if they persevered in the faith.'

The return journey to Kabarole was one of successive drenchings from wet grass, storms, and swollen rivers. In negotiating one slippery hill, Miss Hurditch recalled how 'Faithful Apolo insisted on grabbing my arm with such a grip that when it finally lost all power of feeling, a row of bruises presented themselves to prove the conflict passed through.' They arrived back exhilarated after tramping (the bicycles soon came to grief!) something in the region of 120 miles.

At home in Kabarole

In 1902 an English missionary took over Butiti, and Apolo returned to Kabarole. From there, he records, 'I went visiting the churches.'

Fisher tells how all Apolo's training had been in the direction of making him feel that he was a pastor of the Toro Church and responsible for the flock. He also paid tribute to Apolo's holy, consistent life. 'His face is an inspiration, and he is greatly beloved by us all for his simple wholeheartedness and desire to win souls.'[5]

For fifteen years (1900–15) Apolo was a true pastor to the widely scattered sheep in Toro, travelling on foot hundreds of miles each year to visit the churches, where he would stop a day or two, endeavouring to rouse the people and encourage the teachers with special meetings. The burden of his preaching was always that Christ loves each one, of how he died for them and calls them to be his children. The Rev. Anderea Sere also told how he preached against witchcraft and drink. No doubt he knew better than most the destructive powers of both, but it appears he was not the denouncing type of preacher; it is told how he strove rather to bring people to Christ above all else, as it was only when they had a growing vision of goodness and holiness that drunkenness and witchcraft would in time lose their appeal. He was always quick to encourage those who were trying. 'I praised them for their perseverance and faith.'

It is said that his big flat feet with spread-out toes enabled him to walk anywhere. He never wore shoes. Anderea, who went on many missionary journeys with Apolo, recalls how these were always happy occasions. There would be much singing as the little column of porters wound its way along the twisting paths—'they would go miles and miles singing one or two verses of a hymn'. Apolo always greeted strangers, especially the women and children. On these journeys they never went armed with spears. Sometimes the porters carried clubs as a protection against wild animals, but 'there was never any time for hunting, Apolo walked fast and the others were expected to keep up'. Anderea told of one trip to Lake Edward when they were all in canoes going to visit an island and a storm blew up; these can be very sudden and dangerous. They all sang and the storm abated. The people were very surprised and asked them to sing again.

Year in and year out for the rest of his life Apolo was following the winding paths, through forest and plain and mountain, carrying the message that burned in his heart, fanning the little flames of Christian life that in some places burned brightly, while in others they merely smouldered or had gone out. Each year in his diary he records these journeys and a glance at the Baptismal Register for Toro will also show to what extent he moved about the country.

Nevertheless his home at Kabarole was a centre of life and hospitality; at all times there were visitors. Fisher mentions how Apolo's house was always full between services when the teachers from the outlying churches had come in to Kabarole for their annual conference.[6] Again Fisher writes, 'The public road only separates his house from mine, and I can hear him at all hours of the day teaching hymns and praying with the people, and doing pastoral work. At sunrise and at sunset Apolo gathers everyone around, including passers-by, to join him in morning and evening prayer, using the psalm of the day. He reads his own verse in a loud voice and the congregation's in a low voice, just to encourage those not quite sure of the words, never forgetting the "gloria", which they sing for all they are worth.'[7]

Erisaniya Munubi, who had lived in Apolo's household for five years as a young boy, tells us that Apolo had a square house with several rooms, built in European fashion, with mud and wattle walls, a thatched roof and earth floor smoothed over with cowdung. He always had a number of young boys living with him who worked for him as servants when they were not attending school. In later years, when he had more rooms, both girls and boys lived in his home; the former had their own room and were carefully supervised. Apolo was very good to widows and women who had been deserted. They also joined his household, and occupied an outside house. They would do the cooking for the household and cultivate his garden.

This household cluster of women and young people and always one or more visitors followed the traditional social pattern, but in Apolo's home it appears to have been purified. The strength of his personality kept control, and where he was concerned no breath of scandal ever tainted his reputation as a man of chastity. Erisaniya said: 'Apolo's house was a holy house; you would feel that you must not do anything wrong in that place.' Apolo looked after his children like a father; those who did not do their work properly had to do it a second time, and boys who were repeatedly disobedient were on occasion beaten with the rib of a banana leaf. Erisaniya himself had a beating for not taking the jiggers out of his toes after repeated warning. (The presence of these burrowing pests in the feet would give rise to festering sores if not removed.)

It seems Apolo was not easily provoked. In later years he acquired a bicycle, and on one occasion when visiting he asked Erisaniya to pump up his flat tyre. Erisaniya stupidly went on pumping until it burst. Apolo laughed and said, 'I thought someone was shooting us! But you will now have to carry the load home.'

His patience and love with young people is also illustrated by the following story. Kacope came from Butiti, where he had been baptized by Apolo, who was his godfather. In later years he attended school in Fort Portal. One day when Apolo was visiting, Kacope came round to greet his godfather, who was busy talking to another priest on the veranda about some important matters. The priest waved Kacope away and said, 'Can't you see we are busy? Go away!' But Apolo, looking round, saw who it was and called Kacope to him, and taking both his hands in his said he was busy now, but could see him later. Kacope went away soothed in spirit instead of feeling resentful, as he would otherwise have done.

A rather charming story is told of Apolo about this time. A consignment of dolls had been sent to the lady missionaries at Kabarole for distributing to deserving children—those who consistently came to school clean and washed! After the children's initial fear of them there was a great demand for 'a child that causes play', both from children and adults alike. 'Apolo, our faithful native deacon, a confirmed bachelor, asked me in secret if men ever played with dolls, and beamed with satisfaction as he most triumphantly carried one off, peacefully sleeping.'[8] It is not told what he did with it, but one can hazard a guess that it was kept in his house to entertain many a small visitor.

Apolo greatly admired the flower gardens planted by the English missionaries around their homes. Seeds imported from England grow readily in the dark loam of Toro, and he soon had a neat flower garden around his own house. He also planted fruit trees to provide for the future; the large mango trees near the present church hall at Kabarole mark the site of Apolo's old garden.

Life in the community at Kabarole was a busy coming and going. 'The Christians of those days were an active Christian society— everything they discussed together. The Mukama came down to morning prayers and Bible reading.'[9] In all things the Mukama showed a sincere desire to be a leader and example to his people. When a small hospital was established at Kabarole, Kasagama set about banishing the widespread fear of anaesthesia by himself undergoing a minor operation under an anaesthetic. Also the children of the Royal household were the first to be vaccinated against smallpox. Mrs Fisher tells how almost daily, with a large company of retainers and an armed bodyguard at the front and rear, the Mukama rode down on his horse, a fine majestic figure, followed by the *Katikiro* and other important chiefs, to learn the wisdom of God.

When the drum beat for Sunday services Kasagama was nearly

always at his place in the church to join with his people in prayer and worship. Besides encouraging his young men and chiefs to offer themselves as teachers, he saw to it that land was available for the churches to be self-supporting.[10] The African clergy were given a village or two by the Mukama for their material support. Apolo received the villages of Butinda and Muboku; they 'belonged' to him for his lifetime and he was entitled to the taxes. It is told that instead of collecting these Apolo got the people to work for him when necessary, at cultivating or building. A church was built in each village and he had a special care for 'his people'.

Toro was becoming 'civilized'. The Mukama had built himself a mud-brick two-storied house with an outside staircase. On the ground floor there was a large reception room, the walls and ceiling gaily hung with bright printed calico strips sewn together, upon which were stuck large coloured Bible pictures illustrating the life of Christ. The floor was spread with grass mats and leopard skins. A flower garden adorned the precincts of the house.

Old customs were dying. The custom of women feeding apart from the men in the Mukama's household had gone; husband and wife would dine together and entertain in European style. The newly introduced games of football and tennis provided interest and occupation. The festivals of Christmas and Easter were becoming a joyful feature in the life of the community. Sports were organized on high days and holidays by the mission, and the great and most humble joined in them with enthusiasm.

The progress of a priest

In June 1903 Apolo travelled to Kampala, where he was ordained a priest in the newly completed brick and thatch cathedral on Namirembe hill.

'It was the policy of Bishop Tucker in the early days of the mission to ordain men to the Ministry who had given evidence of Christian character and power of leadership, although their intellectual attainment might be small. This was the only means by which it was possible to make the sacraments available for the large numbers who were pressing into the Church. Apolo was one of these. He never had the opportunity of theological training in the ordinary sense of the term, but his devotion, his saintliness of life, his understanding of men, and his missionary passion have made him one of the strongest spiritual forces in the diocese.'[11]

Fisher writes of him, 'When I first met him in 1896 I thought he was simple, but now, after living with him for years I think him one of the most remarkable men I know. He is never without a "gloria" on his lips . . . And of his work one cannot speak too highly. He is greatly loved and respected by natives and Europeans alike. He would not perhaps be considered a great preacher, but he certainly is a great teacher, and a true soul-winner. He is very keen to learn, and spends all his spare time in self-improvement of some kind or another. The Thirty-nine Articles he committed to memory in less than a month, and on receiving a copy of the *Katikiro* of Buganda's new history of that country, he stayed up all night reading it, so good was this feast of new literature.'[12]

The Rev. T. B. Johnson writes of Apolo at this time also: 'A few sentences of admiration from my fellow missionaries gave me my first insight into the character of this man, whom I have since come to regard as second only to the King in influence.' At their first meeting Apolo with great pertinacity insisted on the new arrival learning the Lunyoro greetings.[13]

The work of a priest can be appreciated by looking closer at the Church in Toro at this time. On the credit side, the years 1901–3 showed the greatest nominal response (judging from the baptismal statistics) to Christian teaching. The Mukama was now well established and his principal chiefs and their followings made a mass movement into the Church. There was also a feeling of patriotism; they were going to be a distinctive people. The British civil administration had established peace and brought prosperity and trade, and the guidance and teaching of the missionaries gave confidence and enabled them to take advantage of these settled conditions.

In turn the Toro Church was encouraged to emulate the Church in Buganda in recognizing its responsibilities to those still living in darkness, and people in the villages who asked for a teacher were expected to build a church, as well as a house for the teacher and to supply him with food. By the end of 1902 there were eighty-eight of these outstations.[14]

Also in 1902 the first women teachers were sent out two by two into the nearby villages to teach reading, to visit and stir up the baptized women to visit in turn the surrounding gardens. Out of the ten sent, six returned immediately to their stations after the first settled period of six months' work. One of the important women of the Mukama's household, Hana Kageye, went to distant Ankole. 'Hana Kageye was in old times one of the worst because most capable women in the country; she had become one of the most potent factors for good . . . On hearing that the Mugabe of Ankole had at last accepted Christian teaching in his country she volunteered to go and teach the women of the royal family, for, as a woman of considerable status she would have more influence with these proud and secluded people than someone of more humble origins.'[15]

Increasing quantities of gospels in Lunyoro, hymns, catechisms and reading sheets likewise helped the work considerably.[16]

However, the newly embraced faith was for ever being assailed by the backward pull of heathenism, and now came the more subtle and insidious temptations of increased prosperity and ease. The introduction of rupees to replace the cumbersome cowrie-shell currency made the acquisition of wealth easier. The men were beginning to drift to the growing townships to seek work for money wages, and the Christian communities in the villages were being broken up. The women who were left behind were exposed to great temptations. Many teachers regarded their work in the Church merely as a phase in their life. Fisher wrote: 'The idea is growing that a Christian, when confirmed, may be a teacher for a year or so, and then he is free to "rest" or trade, or do as he likes, but one has to remember that the young men so lately picked out of the filth and mud of heathenism could hardly have a high standard of life's responsibilities.'

The temperament of the people was feckless, but seen against the background of the past history it was hardly surprising.

Kasagama remarked, 'The Batoro are good at beginning, but they cannot finish.' This was seen on all sides in unfinished houses, fences, and ill-kept roads. Maddox remarked, 'Toro has accepted Christianity almost without question, and people come continually to be baptized without realizing their need of a Saviour, some learn this later, but how many never find this out? No wonder their religion is empty and useless.'[17]

The cases of grievous sin and falling back among baptized Christians could also be traced to the lack of shepherding by older and experienced pastors. More Apolos were needed! Expansion had been so fast and far flung that the striplings sent out as teachers too often proved incompetent. But at the same time Johnson was able to report 'real progress was to be discerned deep down . . . a more thoughtful spirit in the church council and a graver anxiety among them on behalf of the individual Christian who may have fallen into sin. The Christian standard and atmosphere of life is, I believe, improving'.[18]

The rapid and shallow conversion of the country now called for the most careful supervision. Tomasi Ndahura tells how 'Apolo used to worry because there were not sufficient or suitable teachers for the work, he would call the teachers together to talk to them and he prayed with them. Some were really changed, and some went on as they were, but he would not give up'.

Apolo's constant visiting and concern for all people, who, in great weakness, and surrounded by much that was dark and degrading, were yet trying to obey the voice of God as they understood it, was a factor that had a great effect on church attendance. To know that someone cared about their welfare was something of immense importance. The English missionaries also leaned upon Apolo for his advice and his ability to understand and handle the people, who were in very many ways still a mystery to them.

Besides his single-minded devotion to winning people to Christ, his standards of cleanliness and order and hard work were a worthy example. His own clothing and the church vestments were kept spotless. He was a builder of churches, working with his hands and instructing the people in building rectangular mud-walled churches. Beauty and reverence in church services was very important to him; he did not approve of the tendency to do away with all church ornaments, which was manifest in the Protestant Church in some parts of Uganda as a reaction against the Roman Church. He always placed a cross on the altar and grew flowers to decorate the sanctuary. Apolo was laughed at for his flower garden. 'He has learnt the English way!' But in time, due to his influence, many of the country churches had neatly cut grass and flower beds surrounding them. Another of his practical measures was to plant the quick-growing eucalyptus trees around the churches in Toro and Mboga, so that straight poles and beams would be handy for repairing or rebuilding when the need arose. To this day in Toro groups of these trees mark the sites of many churches, and at Mboga a handsome avenue of flowering eucalyptus leads up the hill to the church, and large mangoes and red-flowering spathodea grace the mission compound.

Apolo was becoming known outside Toro. On his annual visits to Kampala for the Synod he visited Christian centres on the way and was asked to preach at churches and schools in Buganda when he was at the capital.

In 1912 Bishop Willis (Bishop Tucker retired in 1911) made a flying visit to western Uganda. Apolo records, 'He and nine others arrived in Toro on bicycles, we saw this wonder . . . I accompanied the Bishop and we visited the county chiefs.' In June of that year Apolo went to the Synod in Kampala and accomplished the journey in four days instead of the usual ten or fifteen. He had obviously borrowed a bicycle!

By 1913 a review of the Church in Toro shows how the mission station at Kabarole had grown. Medical work had begun in 1903, and a large brick hospital was completed in 1911. A fine new brick church with an iron roof had been entirely built by the Christians under the supervision of Maddox. There were boarding and day schools for both boys and girls, and industrial work for women was supervised by Miss Allen. There were now two English and three African clergymen, together with 120 teachers, to minister to this enormous area. A large class for training the teachers was kept going. 'We try to impress upon all our teachers the urgent necessity of visiting from house to house, thus keeping in touch with the home life of the Christians, and learning their special difficulties.' The review also mentions that the Mukama Daudi Kasagama 'is still as keen as ever he was for the advancement of Christ's kingdom in Toro'.[19]

In January 1913 Apolo bought a bicycle for 135 rupees. It was a lady's bicycle. These models were generally preferred by men who wore the long kanzu, which made it difficult to mount a bicycle with a cross-bar. From now on the time spent in travelling would be cut considerably, provided the bicycle did not break down too often; but as yet roads were rough and many places still only accessible on foot. This bicycle was very precious to Apolo and he forbade his boys to ride it.

In April Apolo went to Buganda to attend a course for the African clergy held at the boys' school at Budo. 'The clergy numbered about 37. Five English people addressed us . . . The course covered 25 days.'

Butiti 1913–15

'30 June: They sent me to Butiti.' Over the years Butiti had become a pastorate centre for eastern Toro. Apolo was to remain here for two and a half years.[20]

After journeying to Buganda for the Synod in July, Apolo straightway went visiting the churches in his new pastorate. Each month there are lists of places visited. At the larger centres like Kitagweta, Butara, and Ngongi he would stay some days to examine people for baptism and give Holy Communion. At others he would just gather the people and preach to them, as well as visiting the cattle kraals of the Bahuma between Butiti and Nkoma. He told them, 'It is your work to teach all the other Bahuma.' He wrote of these journeys, 'God protected me all the way.'

The entries for Apolo's diary for 1914 read the same as the last six months of 1913. He notes on 21 February: 'I went to Butara, and found many people waiting for me on the road, men, women and children, altogether 90. On Sunday there were 207 people in the church and I preached about Our Father's wish for many to go to Heaven.'

In June, 'I went to Kitagweta to give Holy Communion and told them to be patient in Jesus and He will even give you rain for it had been very dry. I prayed and it rained straight away, and, in that way God made me do that as a miracle.' The failure of the April–June rains had caused widespread famine in Toro and Bunyoro. The extraordinary improvidence of the people made it develop into a much more serious affair than it need have been, as they only plant and reap for their immediate needs and seldom store any surplus against times of drought, and those who do so have their stores robbed as soon as food becomes scarce.[21]

In July Apolo was off to Buganda to attend the missionary council. In September he was again visiting the churches and preaching about God's kingdom, 'That Holy land God wishes to give us . . . How Jesus went to prepare a place in Heaven for us; in that lovely world there will the righteous go and the wicked will not go there.'

In March 1915 he again mentions visiting the cattle kraals of the Bahuma, urging them to continue praying and to keep Sundays.

'15 June: I went to Buganda to attend the Synod.' He then preached at Budo (possibly to an Education Conference held there after the Synod).

After returning to Butiti 'we chose the rural parish councils'. In August he was again visiting the Bahuma cattle kraals. 'I asked them to go on in earnest belief.'

'6 August. I reached Kitagweta and we held a church council to discuss about teachers' pay. On Sunday after Holy Communion I baptized six people . . . 13 August: I reached Butara. We gathered in church . . . I baptized 3 people and told them that God the Holy Spirit caused the gospels to be written as they were written in the Bible, that they should read it and find out for themselves . . .

I came away from Butiti on 9 December 1915 and went to Kabarole.'

NOTES

[1] H. E. Maddox, 'Butiti, Toro', *Mengo Notes*, June 1901, pp. 57–58.

[2] A. B. Fisher, *Mengo Notes*, August 1901, p. 67.

[3] Ruth B. Fisher, *On the Borders of Pygmyland* (1905), p. 109.

[4] Fisher, *ibid.*, pp. 110–11.

[5] A. B. Fisher, Annual Letter, November 1902, C.M.S. Archives.

[6] A. B. Fisher, 'Conference of Teachers in Toro', *Mengo Notes*, September 1900, p. 20.

[7] A. B. Fisher, Annual Letter, Toro, 30 November 1902, C.M.S. Archives.

[8] Ruth B. Fisher, *op. cit.*, p. 81.

[9] Information from the Rev. Yosia Kamuhigi.

[10] Ruth B. Fisher, *op. cit.*, p. 64.

[11] From a reference to Apolo's life and work in the *Church Overseas*, October 1933, p. 356.

[12] A. B. Fisher, Annual Letters for 1901 and 1902, C.M.S. Archives.

[13] T. B. Johnson, *Tramps Around the Mountains of the Moon*, pp. 51–52.

[14] A. B. Fisher, Annual Letter, Toro 1902, C.M.S. Archives.

[15] Johnson, *op. cit.*, pp. 195–6.

[16] See Lunyoro book sales for 1901.

[17] H. E. Maddox, Annual Letter, Toro, 29 September 1903, C.M.S. Archives.

[18] T. B. Johnson, Annual Letter, Toro, 30 November 1903, C.M.S. Archives.

[19] 'Review of the Missionary District of Toro', *Uganda Notes*, July 1913, pp. 164–9.

[20] Apolo had also been stationed at Butiti for a short time in 1904. The Annual Report from Toro for 1904 records that while he was there 'attendance at Sunday services doubled'. It is also of interest that in 1905 Apolo accompanied two of the European missionaries (Rev. H. W. Tegart and H. E. Maddox) on a climb to the glaciers of Ruwenzori. 'An Ascent of Mount Ruwenzori', *Uganda Notes*, June 1905, pp. 86–89.

[21] H. A. Brewer, 'Hoima during 1914–15', *Uganda Notes*, July 1915, p. 432.

9

THE DECLINE AND REVIVAL OF
THE MBOGA CHURCH

A flock without a shepherd

THE decline of the Church at Mboga is a sad story and resembles that of other isolated Christian communities at this stage of the Church's growth. It is difficult to define just what constituted the Church at Mboga. It was a weak Church. Of those baptized only a small portion persevered. The quick reaching out in the beginning for this new faith and a response to its demands was made very often spontaneously and unthinkingly. The new life presented by the gospels was a revelation to these people, but they found it very difficult to relate it to their own lives. It was only when those, who, faced with decisions that deeply affected their lives or by a sudden conflict of loyalties, could make a deliberate stand for the truth as they understood it, that the Church began to grow, inwardly and often imperceptibly. A corporate conscience is of slow growth, but it began to be manifest in the leaders who formed the church council, which was largely drawn from the first thirteen Christians to be baptized at Mboga. They had withstood persecution in the enthusiasm of their new love and their loyalty to Apolo. It would also seem that Apolo had taught them well; he himself had grasped the reality of Christ and showed this clearly in his life and teaching.

The extreme difficulty for the Church to maintain its identity in a pagan society, to 'come out and be separate' and act independently, can only be appreciated when it is understood how completely the people were subject to the powers of the unseen world, of magic and spirit possession, as well as the more visible powers of chiefs and clan and tribal customs. To leap the gulf between a polygamous society and one based on Christian morality was immeasurably hard for an African Christian, and his resolve was so often sapped by drunkenness.

Besides these inherent difficulties Mboga suffered a complete isolation from any other Christian community; their nearest ordained priest was sixty miles away and he could only visit them once or twice a year. The catechists sent over from Toro as teachers were ill equipped for their immensely important work of preaching, teaching, evangelizing the heathen, and shepherding the faithful. The influence of the teacher with both chief and people was all important, and when perhaps he was faced with opposition, or more often mere inertia and dullness, a weak teacher would lose his zeal and remain content merely to read services and teach reading, and do nothing to reach the heathen or reclaim backsliders.

Political troubles also bedevilled the work at Mboga. After the area had again come within the British sphere of influence in 1901 pending the recommendations of a Boundary Commission, large numbers of different tribes migrated from the Congo side of the border to settle near Mboga 'because the British did not plunder'. This mingling of people and the fact that Mboga was becoming the centre for the rubber trade[1], which tended in turn to scatter people in pursuit of easy money, made church work difficult. Added to this, the vices of a trading community of Indians and Swahilis did not improve the character of the place.

Apolo visited Mboga in 1905 with Dr and Mrs Bond. They received a hearty welcome, but found the people in straits for food as a long drought had caused famine. In two days 550 people flocked to get medicine from the doctor. A congregation of 260 attended the Sunday service and there were eighty communicants, but no adults for baptism. A visit to Bubogo showed that the chief Kwezi was 'reading' with his sons and some of his people; presumably a Christian teacher was living there. The old chief was polygamous and had not yet considered baptism. The missionaries noted a colony of Babira at this place, who had recently come across the border. They then visited Bulei where they were received with great insolence by the chief Opedi, who had at one time been 'reading', but had given it up. Here was an evil settlement of Swahili, Baganda, and Arab traders.

Nearby a colony of Bahuku had taken refuge.[2] The missionaries visited them also and recorded that they were cannibals and corpse-eaters. 'When their people die, they do not eat their own relations, but invite others to do so, expecting in return to be invited to partake of a feast when their friends' relations die.'[3] The need for someone to evangelize these degraded tribes was great. Apolo led the missionary party back to Toro by way of Bwamba, preaching to the people in the villages they passed through. Dr Bond records how Apolo spoke to them: 'He told them that we had one Maker and Saviour of all, Baamba, Baganda, and European alike . . . and he spoke to them of the Lamb of God who taketh away the sins of the world, asking them questions from time to time to see if they understood. When he asked them to kneel in prayer some of them began to laugh, yet they did as he asked them.'

In September 1907 Apolo records: 'They sent me to Mboga. I found very few people reading. God gave me great strength to give myself to prayer, because my custom is to pray a lot secretly in my house and in the church, thus I prayed. I feel God calling many. Let us start slowly and afterwards more quickly.' Apolo spent four months here and one has little doubt that a response to his energetic and loving care was immediate. But it is evident that the disruption of the community and lack of shepherding had sapped the vitality of this church, and after Apolo returned to Toro they sank again into inertia.

In January 1909 Apolo went there again, and described very aptly the state of the church when he said, 'I found the church in the long grass and dug it out.' He set the people to work at once. 'I encouraged the Christians to clear a road to the church.' He seems to have paid a second visit, for in May he mentions visiting Bulei, 'where they refused to believe on Christ'. He then went to

Bulega 'and found they had a church and a teacher—Paulo Rwa-kaikara'. This teacher had been sent across from the mission at Hoima in Bunyoro, as an effort was being made from there to evangelize the country west of Lake Albert.

Apolo did not visit Mboga again until November 1910. He briefly states that he found only thirty people assembled in church. In February 1911 he again went to Mboga, but only records that he had some of his property stolen while he was there. But this was the year when Mboga was officially handed over to Belgium and fresh handicaps were placed on missionary work from British Uganda. The Mukama Paulo Tabaro fled to Toro because he feared the Belgians, who again made his cousin Sulemani Karemesa chief of Mboga, but subject to Bomera,[4] whom they made senior chief of the whole area between Irumu and the Semliki river. The warlike Balega in the hills north of Mboga greatly resented the transfer of their territory to Belgium and the imposition of Bomera's authority.[5] As a result they rose in rebellion and killed Bomera and his entourage. Exaggerated tales of the Balega rising, which included the dramatic sacking of Mboga, reached Toro, and Apolo was supposed to have organized relief for these allegedly stricken people,[6] but there is no evidence of this.

Darker days were now to overshadow the Mboga Church. Sulemani Karemesa, at one time a Roman Catholic convert, had reverted to his pagan ways and strongly opposed what remained of the small Christian community, who were now without a teacher, as the Belgians would allow no entry of persons from Uganda. Paulo Tabaro was, however, later allowed to return to live ignominiously among his people.

No more is heard of Mboga for the next four years, until Apolo was sent over there in December 1915 to see how things were. 'They were very glad to see me and 100 people came to meet me on the way, Paulo Tabaro too was there . . . I found the spiritual life of the church very low . . . many whom I had known had gone back, the church was falling down, the congregation had lost all heart.' He at once set them rebuilding the church. On 27 December he returned to Kabarole, where, he wrote significantly 'we had a meeting'.

Apolo had now worked twenty years in Toro, and had asked for a year's leave in Buganda, which had been readily granted him, but he was so greatly concerned over the condition of the Christians at Mboga that 'with tears in his eyes he begged Rev. A. B. Lloyd . . . to let him spend his holiday among these people. The request was granted, and the intended visit to Buganda was indefinitely posponed'.[7] 'I did not take up my leave, for God sent me to Mboga, so that I did not stop doing His work of changing people's hearts to hear Him.'

Enemies of the Gospel

On 4 January 1916 Apolo set off from Kabarole and arrived at Mboga on the 6th.[8] On the 10th: 'Four Belgians came to Mboga, the Mukama Sulemani Karemesa sent for me, and abusing me to the Belgians accused me of saying his country belonged to the British.' However, on interrogating Apolo the Belgians could find no fault with him.

Apolo laments: 'When I reached Mboga, I found some of the Christians possessed by an evil spirit. Some were practising witchcraft. Some had three wives, some two, and there was too much drinking of beer. I was very much worried by these evil practices amongst the Christians at Mboga.'

Apolo had a considerable task to salvage the Christian community, but undaunted he set about building a new church and a house for himself and clearing the ground for a garden. He soon had the people rallying around him and helping with the work. Nasani tells how 'the men and women worked together at the building, the women fetched water for puddling the clay, the men went to the forest for trees and did the thatching. Ibrahimu was working on the roof when he fell to the ground and was knocked unconscious, the people thought he was dead and started wailing, but Apolo quieted them, and Ibrahimu soon recovered'. His recovery was attributed to Apolo's presence.

Parents began to bring their boys and girls to learn to read, and soon Apolo's household took on the customary 'cluster' pattern; young boys and girls came to serve him and be taught; they lived in his house and went about everywhere with him. 'They had found a kind friend with whom they liked to be,' said Peradasi.

On 5 March Apolo was able to record: 'Paulo Tabaro left off drinking, and also Jamesi Diti, Ibrahimu Katalibara, Firipo Karema, Zakiya Katamara, Elizabeti Ruhubya.'

The Mukama Sulemani, however, continued to oppose Apolo. He feared his influence and resented the fact that Paulo Tabaro was his keen supporter. 'He wants to bring back my brother.⁹ He smuggles cattle and ivory over to Toro.' Apolo, it is said, took little notice of these slanders and just went on in his quiet way. But the following entry in his diary shows that Sulemani's conduct was causing him some concern. 5 April: 'Sulemani Karemesa captured Malyamu Bomero and gave her away to the Belgians after they had asked him for a woman to marry.'

Apolo openly censured Sulemani's behaviour. Tomasi tells how 'one Sunday in church, Apolo spoke out boldly about him, rebuking his conduct, he said "Sulemani has turned his back on God, and God will turn His back on him". Apolo had no fear of chiefs . . . and Sulemani was quite in awe of him'.

In Apolo's diary we have the following entry: 'And I prayed with all the Christians saying "O God look down upon us miserable creatures, without a good ruler in this country of the Congo. May you take away this bad chief from us and make haste to help us", and another time we prayed saying, "O God, the Father, Son and Holy Spirit, we put forth to you this person, so that you may do to him whatever you wish, whether to take him away or to let him live and convert him, for if you do not interfere, he is going to lead many astray and kill them". In this God the Father, Son and Holy Spirit helped us, and the Mukama Sulemani Karemesa died soon after.' He died in August of that year; it was said he had leprosy.

Nasani said 'that in spite of all the women Sulemani had, he had no children, and when he was dying he called Paulo Tabaro and said "You have two children, give me one, and he shall inherit the kingdom when I die." His brother gave him Enoke and when Sulemani died, Enoke became the Mukama'.

Apolo's civilizing influence

On his return from a visit to the Synod in June, Apolo brought a box of eucalyptus trees from Toro to plant at Mboga. He was essentially practical and orderly. His civilizing influence was soon to be seen in the neat church and teachers' house with its well-stocked garden. He planted grass borders and flower beds around the church; these flowers were used in a delightful way for welcoming visitors, who would be greeted by the schoolchildren lining the road waving bunches of flowers tied on to the end of long reeds.

In matters of hygiene Apolo taught the people not to foul the clear-running stream that flowed through Mboga, but to dig latrines away from their water supply, to keep themselves clean and to report and isolate infectious diseases. Tomasi tells how he taught them to sew. 'The kanzus had to be carefully made and decorated with the red stitch as they are in Uganda!'

Later in the year the Belgian officials visited Mboga and were greatly impressed with the church buildings and well-laid out site.

The year 1916 ends on a triumphant note: 'At present many people have been converted and they regularly come to church and confess their sins. In all these things, it is God who helps us.'

On 12 April 1917: 'I went to Bulei to build a church there.' (This was the first movement outwards from Mboga.) Bulei is some five or six miles north of Mboga and had been the head-quarters of the evil sub-chief Opedi. A chief called Nyabongo was now resident there.

'7 June: A Roman Catholic priest of great cleverness known in the country came, and said that the Protestant religion has no truth in it.' He also accused Apolo of being an agent of the Mukama Kasagama of Toro. 'He said these things before Enoke and the chiefs at Mboga' (including Nyabongo and Kituku).

Early in July Apolo visited Toro for the annual teachers' meeting. When he returned he found that Enoke and the chiefs had been converted to the Roman Catholic religion.

'28 July: I became very ill for eight days. I preached in the church with great patience hoping that the kind God would help us and take away the burden from us.'

In August Apolo was over in Toro for another meeting and then went on to 'his' village of Butinda to supervise the rebuilding of the church. The trees which Apolo planted are standing there today.

'I reached Mboga on 15 September and found them still in peace.' '18 September: I sent teachers to Bulei, Samisoni Kabururu and Feliamu Diti, to carry on God's work, for He is almighty who enables anything to be done.'

'5 November: I went to Irumu [sixty miles away], the city of the Bazungu [Europeans of the Congo], to get a letter of authority, that I might continue to work in Mboga. God helped me and they agreed to give it, they were happy to give it to me.' In all the years he was in the Congo Apolo was helped and respected by the Belgian administration.

On his return journey from Irumu, Apolo visited the homes of two Bambuba families of his acquaintance. One couple he baptized. They were possibly freed slaves or the relatives of slaves of the Banyamboga and had thus been taught in Apolo's church. Many forest folk who had come to Mboga while it was still within the British sphere of influence had 'sold' their children to the Banyamboga as slaves in exchange for food and ground to cultivate. Nasani explained: 'These slaves became a kind of currency, that could be exchanged for a plot of potatoes, a boy or a girl as needed, not that they were ill used, for they lived with the people, but they were in servitude.'

Apolo made a point of teaching and encouraging these people, even in the teeth of opposition from their masters. 'The Gospel is for all men.' As it was, when he began to evangelize in the forest these Bambuba slaves came forward as interpreters. (All the forest people had a working knowledge of each other's language.)

In December Apolo was taken ill. 'I have never been sick like this before—there was Holy Communion, but I could not celebrate.' However, he was well enough to walk the sixty arduous miles to Toro for the district councils at the end of the month.

On 2 January 1918, 'I arrived back at Mboga, the Rev. A. B. Lloyd came to visit us with Dr Sharp.'

In February there seems to have been much sickness at Mboga; Apolo himself had ulcers on his head and legs. 'I could not sleep. I left it all with the All Powerful One.'

'8 April: I went to chief Kituku for permission to teach his people. [Kituku's village was about 10 miles north of Mboga.] He refused, as he feared the Roman Catholics would accuse him to the Belgians and he would be removed from his chieftainship. So I left him.'

In June, Apolo went to Toro to meet the Bishop. During his absence conflict broke out between the Christian community and the Mukama Enoke. Isaaka Aliguma, a leading Christian, who found Enoke with his brother's wife, rashly gave him a beating. Enoke then sent his men to arrest Isaaka, who was beaten severely and tied up. He was sent for trial to Irumu on a charge of being rebellious and for not paying the Belgian taxes. There he received fifteen lashes and was released.

When Apolo returned from Toro and heard what had happened he questioned everyone carefully, and decided the fault was with Enoke. Nasani tells how Apolo sent a message to Enoke, saying these three things:

'Your father first began to fight against the Church. He lifted his arm to strike it down.

'You are a child of the Church, and you have done the same thing. In raising your arm against the Church you will be overcome.

'You will leave your kingdom, and you will take hold of a hoe, and with your hands you will dig potatoes.'

Enoke was considerably in awe of Apolo and his interference with the Protestant Christians appears to have subsided. However, two years later (1922) in a state of drunkenness, he attempted to assault a Belgian official who was staying at the nearby rest camp. He was arrested and spent six months in prison at Irumu. On this occasion Apolo wrote in his diary: 'I had warned the Mukama about his excessive drinking, and said God might see fit to punish him. He is now a prisoner. Surely God is giving him a chance to be taught and to understand what he is doing, for He loves him very much.'

Tomasi tells how eventually, in 1925, Enoke fought with his father Paulo Tabaro, and was arrested by the Belgians for stealing ivory. The Belgians removed him from his chieftainship 'and he ran away to Toro where he is still alive and indeed digs potatoes on his food plot. The Government saw that Paulo Tabaro was upright, and reinstated him. This was a great help to Apolo, whom he helped in many ways, by visiting and teaching'.

'In January 1919 God blessed us in the Church, lots and lots of people came to read and pray, and to learn to write on slates and pieces of paper. In this way God was very good to us, in sending people for His religion.

'12 May: I took 20 people from Mboga to Toro to be confirmed by the Bishop. In that journey God helped me very much, not to be ill and weak, not to be wet through with rain, and to meet no dangers on the road through the devil, such as quarrelling and things like that the devil brings, and for not finding any animals on the road. Lots of mosquitoes got into the shelter in which we slept at night, but God sent a strong wind and blew them away. It was a wonderful thing to be able to sleep well, without danger. God the Father, and His Son Jesus Christ and the Holy Spirit be praised.

'25 June: A Belgian official, Zitoni, came to Mboga and I paid my hut tax to him. He heard the words of this place (requests and other needs) and removed the settlers (no one may move about the Congo without permission). We were very angry with him because of this, but he would not listen to our reasons. These families were sent back to where they had originally come from and three other families sent to take up their homes and gardens.

'4 August: I set out for Kampala to attend the Synod and the consecration of the great new brick cathedral. [13 September 1919.]

'3 October: I began to build a school at Mboga . . . there were 10 workmen and each was paid 6 francs. The building was finished on 31 October. Petero Kamihanda gave a bullock to the church when he died. I sold it for 30 rupees (60 francs). This Christian, though he was dying, did not forget God who created him—the Christians who are alive should take thought for what they can give to God.'

This school received the support and approval of the Belgian Administration, who provided desks and supplies of paper, pencils, and chalk. On 18 April 1921 Apolo records how the Belgian Commissioner came to inspect the school. 'He visited the whole station and complimented us on it. This Commissioner spread the news of the school in every place he visited in the area. This helped the work and made a great demand for teachers.'

NOTES

[1] Rubber was collected from four species of Landolphia (Apocynaceae) vine growing in the forest. John Mahon, 'Hints on Rubber Collecting', *Uganda Notes*, June 1902, pp. 41–43.

[2] See p. 123.

[3] Dr A. Bond, 'Itineration to Mboga and District', *Uganda Notes*, September 1905, pp. 138–42.

[4] Bomera was related to the royal house of Bunyoro.

[5] The pastoral Banyoro had held uneasy sway over the Balega for generations. The Balega are agricultural people of Sudanic origin.

[6] A. B. Lloyd, *Apolo of the Pygmy Forest*, pp. 37–39.

[7] *Uganda Notes*, October 1916, pp. 142–3.

[8] Apolo never took his bicycle to Mboga; it would have been useless to him there. He left it at Kabarole to use on his annual journeys to the Synod at Kampala.

[9] Paulo Taboro was his cousin. The term 'brother' covered all male relatives of the same generation.

10

THE GOOD NEWS TO THE
FOREST PEOPLE

The forest people

THE path to the forest winds through the open grasslands
above Mboga, from where, on a clear day, the great range
of Ruwenzori is seen to the south-east. Ten miles westwards the
path plunges into the gloom of the forest and soon becomes a mere
tunnel, where a man can scarcely walk upright. Fallen tree trunks
impede his passage and tangled creepers add to the struggle. Constant storms and lack of sun makes this world beneath its great
canopy of foliage both cold and uninviting.

Impenetrable and hostile to the outside world, the forest has
proved a kindly refuge for one of the most ancient remnants of man-
kind. The Pygmies or Bambuti have lived their simple hunting and
gathering life in this environment for perhaps many thousands of
years, and their happy and dependent relationship with the forest
they express in song and dance. The impact of the migrant Bantu
tribes who later settled on the fringes of the forest brought little
change to the Pygmy way of life. The forest was hostile to the
agricultural and pastoral people from the plains and savannah
country; it was an element to be fought against, to be cleared and
cut down; and the enemies of the forest were the enemies of the
Pygmy. However, the Pygmy learnt to move easily from one world
to the other, forming arbitrary associations with his Bantu neighbours for purposes of trade or amusing diversion, but once he

returned to his forest life he reverted to his ancient ways.[1]

In the Mboga area the Pygmies associate with the agricultural Bambuba with whom they trade meat and ivory for bananas or yams, salt, iron arrowheads, spears and knives, helping themselves without permission to these commodities and leaving the meat in exchange. Their association with the 'protecting' tribe is often very close, as they acquire both their language and customs and inter-marriage may occur. The Pygmies are considered valuable allies in tribal wars because of their skill as forest trackers and their accuracy with bow and poisoned arrow.

These little hunters and gatherers of the forest are no taller than 4 foot 8 inches, they are lighter coloured than the darker Bantu and often covered with downy hair. The only clothing worn by either sex is a loincloth of bark fibre. They move about in hunting groups of twenty families or more and make their temporary en-campments wherever they intend to stay for a few weeks or months. Their huts are built of a framework of saplings planted in a circle and bent to form a dome, interlaced with creepers and thatched with large leaves; a small hole is left near the ground as an entrance. These flimsy huts are never more than 3 feet high and about 6–9 feet in diameter.

Cohesion among the Pygmies is loose, hunting groups are held together by kinship ties, law and order is a co-operative matter. Quarrels are frequent and often break out over trifling matters, when spears and arrows start flying. But the Pygmies are a charac-teristically humorous and happy people. A very distinctive feature of their life is the song and dance through which they maintain their relationship with the forest, whose well-being and their own are so closely linked.

Although they are intensely cautious and suspicious of strangers and rarely let themselves be seen, they are skilled and fearless hunters. Yusufu Limenya, who has lived amongst them, describes how they hunt the elephant. 'They wait hidden high among the foliage of the trees for the herd to approach, when they have singled out their victim, perhaps a big tusker, one of their number drops to the ground in front of the elephant to attract its attention, while the others swing down and slash the tendons of his hind legs and attempt to spear him in the stomach with their short-handled, broad-bladed spears; as the infuriated beast lashes about they swing back into the trees, but the man in front leaps about in a position of great danger just beyond the reach of the elephant's trunk to divert his attention. The others rush in again for another attack. If the Pygmies are far in the forest they will swarm upon the carcass and eat the meat raw; cooking is a refinement for those who have fire.'

The agricultural neighbours of the Pygmies in this part of the forest are the Bambuba and the Bahuku. Both tribes live in villages on the outskirts of the forest. Their agriculture is of the crudest; crops of millet, beans and cassava being planted haphazardly among the roughly cleared forest stubble; when the ground becomes exhausted the group moves on to clear new ground.

The Bambuba of these parts claim that they originally came from the region of Kisenyi on Lake Albert. At one time the lake rose and they were pushed into higher, less fertile country and then wandered down towards the forest where they came in contact with the Pygmies. The Pygmy likes to tell how the first innocent Bambuba to come to the forest did not know how to procreate their species; the Pygmy it seems soon put that right! Thus the Bambuba claim relationship with the Pygmies. It was also a Pygmy who first gave them fire. He sent his dog off to bring a burning brand from a tree that had been struck by lightning. Thus the Pygmy feels entitled to help himself to the coals of the Bambuba fires; these he wraps in banana leaves and carries smouldering about the forest with him until he needs to make a fire or light his pipe. Likewise the Pygmy helps himself to the bananas in the Bambuba gardens, as he claims he was the first to show a Mumbuba the banana tree, according to the following tale—'The Bambuba were very hungry and complained to the Pygmy that they had nothing to eat. The Pygmy said, "Come, I will show you some food", and he took a man to a banana tree with a fine bunch of fruit hanging on it. He gave the Mumbuba the choice, "Will you take the bunch of fruit or would you like the stump of the tree that will be left?" The

Pygmy really wanted the fruit, which he got, leaving the stump to the other man. The Pygmy went home with his bananas and when he had cooked and eaten them, there was nothing left, but the Mumbuba, although he could not satisfy his immediate hunger planted the stump and eventually had plenty of food. Thus he became an agriculturist.'[2]

The Bahuku closely resemble the Baamba, and in Apolo's day they wore their hair in a shaggy mop of strands twisted with goat's fat, which gave them a particularly wild appearance. These people were alleged to be cannibals and corpse-eaters, the dead being purchased from their relatives for goats.

Groups of cannibal witches also occurred within the tribal groups. Here the taste for human flesh was bound up with the magical means of procuring it.[3] The leader of such a group later came under the influence of one of Apolo's Christian teachers in the forest and was finally baptized in the forest church of Bwakadi by Apolo.

It is claimed by the people of Mboga that the Bahuku also caught strangers venturing into their territory. Yusufu said that all these forest tribes went about in great fear of each other.[4]

Apolo's call

The English missionaries had urged Apolo to take the Gospel to the forest, and now that the church at Mboga was on its feet again the time had come for expansion. Apolo tells how God encouraged him to go to the forest.

'Again in 1921 Christ appeared to me in the form of a man and stood beside me. It was as if I saw a man who was my brother. He said to me, "Go and preach in the forest because I am with you." I answered saying, "Who is speaking to me?" He said, "I Am That I Am; that is my name." When I arose I started on the expedition. When I began they just looked at me. I did not know their language and they did not know mine. I just sat as if I could not do anything, because from of old they said to me, "In the forest there are cannibals." It is a blessing I have been able to teach the slaves who were bought in this forest.

123

'Looking round I saw a man coming who had been baptized as a captive. His friends said of him "This man knows your language. Come and see him." Then this man greeted me and I knew him. He was Yohana (John), and so I found an interpreter and I thanked Jesus.'[5]

'21 April: I went with some of the teachers to the forest, where the Bambuba were at a place called Mugenyi. Ezira Muyombo was left at Kamega, Edwardi went to Bakyetaho. Yasoni Kagurumu took some other teachers into the forest at Banyajawo and they left Yosia Kaburwa and Yafesi Bamuhaga with the Bahuku at Kabebi. Thus we began to teach the Bahuku and Bambuba.'

These 'teachers' were the young men and older boys from the Mboga school. They were weak material, but many of them were faithful in their task through the years.

'22 April: We wrote in our book "God sent us to them". They received the Word quickly . . .

'30 April: I came back, and I prayed that God would answer the prayers of his people with great joy. We prayed daily for those parts of the country.' Apolo called 1921 'the year of the Gospel'.

Again 'We went into the forest to the house of Banyajawo to write down names of those who wished to be baptized. . . . We left them and went to the house of Misango. . . . We went to see Abembi at Budingiri, they asked me for a teacher, we put in the posts for a church there. . . . We were very pleased to see this church among the Bambuba. . . . We went to the house of Wamenga and, God being my helper, we arrived at the house of Sabuna. . . . "Give us, Oh God our Father, to overcome the Bambuba, that they may become Thy people." I prayed with them.' The Banyamboga heartily despised the forest people and would not eat their food. Apolo went among them as a friend, ate their food and slept in their homes; his young teachers often found this difficult.

Bishop Willis and Lloyd visited Mboga at the end of the year. 'We received much strength and heart from their visit.' They toured the forest 'churches' and the Bishop confirmed twenty people at Mboga. They also visited the authorities at Irumu, 'as there were difficulties with the Roman Catholics. We got back to Mboga and the Bishop preached the Gospel to us in many good words'.

It may have been some time during this year that a strange event occurred related by Yoweri Rwakaikara, one of Apolo's boys. Apolo went to Geti, the nearest Belgian administrative post, some thirty miles from Mboga, to get permission to move his teachers about without special permits. This permission was granted, provided Apolo gave each teacher a personal letter to show the itinerating Belgian official. Apolo was accompanied by eight of his boys. 'On the way back, just before reaching Bukiringi, on the side of Budinda hill we met a man of the Balega tribe, carrying his spear. When he was twenty yards away he made directly for Apolo, to attack him, he being unarmed. Apolo continued walking quietly towards him and the man just fell down on the ground. He was so surprised and thwarted that he just got up, turned and ran; we boys were terrified, but we came on quietly to Mboga.'

In 1922 Apolo was made a Canon in the Church of Uganda. The following letter (in Luganda) was pasted into Apolo's diary.

Bishop's House
Kampala
Uganda
22 April 1922

To my brother,

I am very pleased to be able to write to you and to tell you that I have chosen you to be a Canon in the Church of Uganda together with the Rev. N. Mudeka. I have chosen you on account of your great patience and perseverance in Toro and the Congo all these years, and your patience in suffering and persecution for the name of Our Lord, and for taking that name to the heathen. For this reason I consider you worthy of this honour.

May our Father increase upon you the power and strength of the Holy Spirit that He may complete with joy and satisfaction your pilgrimage and the work to which He has called you.

Greet all the Christians at Mboga very much.

I am your brother who loves you.

J. J. Willis[6]

The work in the forest was growing. Small 'churches' were springing up. These simple structures of wattle and daub with thatched roofs, beaten mud floors and gaps left in the walls by way of windows were flimsy structures and fell easily to the ravages of termites and storms. They needed constant rebuilding and repair, just as did the spiritual life of the people. On the walls the teacher would hang his alphabet sheets, and about him on the floor sat a mixed group of learners, saying over the syllables in a sing-song voice; eventually some of them would master consecutive print and be able to read the 'word' for themselves. He would also instruct them in the catechism and Gospel and prepare those who wished it for baptism.

The simple village teacher was himself not far removed from the people he taught; he had to be congruent with their disorganized and timeless way of life. His drum might go to time or it might not; he might be on duty or away visiting. The children drifted in and out of his school and the goats wandered in and ate the reading sheets on the walls. Yet, however haphazard and slow his teaching may have been, he fulfilled an important role. He was the agent of the New Way and his presence in the village was a sign that the people knew they could rise to better things and dimly hoped to do so.[7]

In his travels about the forest, preaching and questioning candidates for baptism, Apolo always had a crowd of young people with him, and they would sing as they wound along the forest paths. Dr Schofield, who went with Apolo on a forest journey, describes how 'he would call first one boy or a girl to walk with him, and one could see that he was teaching them as we all went along'. Apolo was never alone on his travels or in his house. Africans cannot understand anyone liking to be alone. Should anyone be alone they like to be near to 'heal the solitude'.

Lloyd visited the forest churches with Apolo in August, and Apolo baptized those who were ready at Buguje. 'The man Kasoro had been taught by Samisoni Kabururu. He was very courageous and strong in the gospel of Christ. We spent some time with him.'

'15 August: We believed that God would take us out of the

hand of that *Omufumu* (sorcerer).' Perhaps he had put a spell on some member of the congregation at Mboga.

'29 October: We were told that Yonasani had been beaten for preaching the Gospel.

'11 November: The mother of Kituku (chief) came to ask for a teacher to be sent to their place.

'13 November: Chief Kituku himself told me that he did not like the Roman Catholic faith, but preferred the Protestant. He also asked for a teacher.

'26 December: I started my journey to Buganda for the church councils. . . .' Apolo spoke before the Missionary Board about the work in the Congo. 'I was given Shs. 200 towards the work . . . and asked the Bishop for some help in putting the Mboga church in order.'[8]

In 1923 a school-teacher called Lamusi was sent from Toro to help in the school at Mboga. Apolo was headmaster of this school, but the growing work in the forest took him away for part of every month. Apolo appears to have spent some time in Toro during this year, where he received the following letter.

Mboga
2 August 1923

To Canon Apolo Kivebulaya,

How are you getting on Apuli? We greet you very much. First of all we thank God who chose to send you to Mboga, we thank you very much for going to so much trouble about our nation, together with us your children. It is indeed our Father who has done this and you who have helped in it all here at Mboga, and we your children, we will always listen to what you have to say to us, and God will lift from us the great yoke. We will trust Him continually. It is He who is our God, who surpasses all. We will obey Him always together with you, Apuli, we thank you very much for your prayers for us and for our church because we are your children.

It is us your children,
Enoke S.M. 11
Paulo Tabaro
Daudi S. *Katikiro*

127

It is interesting to note that Apolo has received the 'praise' name Apuli. Among the Lunyoro-speaking peoples an *empako* or 'praise' name—there are twelve in all—is given to every child. Outsiders who are loved and welcomed are also generally given an *empako*. These names have no significance and it is now known that they are of Nilotic origin.[9] The fact that the 'praise' name Apuli was so similar to Apolo may have suggested the adoption of this name. It also appears from this letter that the Mukama Enoke was temporarily within the fold.

On 23 February 1924, 'I set out on a visit to the churches, Bukima, Tshabi, Budingiri . . . We took some women teachers, Meri and Yunia. At Tshabi we gathered together about 20 Bahuku.

'We got to the house of Sulemani at Kainama (a settlement of Bakonjo here). We found the teachers Edwardi Byakisaka and Efraimu here. We prayed with about 40 people. We built there a church and a house for the teacher.

'We went to Bwakadi, they besought us for a teacher . . . Everywhere I went in the forest they asked for teachers.'

Each month the entries are much the same; new places in the forest appear. It was good training for the young teachers straightway to pass on their knowledge. A young Muganda, Ruben Kakonge, came to help Apolo in the school at Mboga, so that the ageing priest might give more time to evangelizing the forest folk.

'7 April: I left Mboga to explore a new area to take the name of Our Lord there. Thus it was that God sent me to Bulega country.

'9 April: There I preached to the Balega . . . I was very pleased as many people wanted to hear about the name of Jesus . . . chief Kamachi and his people agreed to have a teacher so I left Levi Balengura to teach them . . . When we found we had been accepted by the people, we prayed the Creator of all things that He would indeed open the door of that country.'

Salt and song

Later in April 'I went to preach to the Pygmies, we found about 15 waiting for us'. Apolo's fame had spread through the forest and now the elusive Pygmies were willing to receive him, although they were still very much afraid of people who wore clothes, because in the past the Arab slave traders of Kilonga Longa had captured the forest tribes.

On 8 September, Apolo went again to preach to the Pygmies. 'They believed and asked for a teacher. I slept with them in their homes. We taught a group of 23. At that time there were about 46 Pygmies being instructed in the forest.

'The chief of the Bambuba did not like my teaching them. He said they were not worth teaching because of their wandering habits and primitive way of life. For my part I was interested to hear what they would have to say for themselves. After talking to them I found them clever and wise. They marry only one wife, they know God as a creator, they know that Eve was taken out of the side of Adam and how they both ate the forbidden fruit and how death came, but they know nothing of a Saviour. It was great fun to stay with these Bambuti people. We ate meat and sweet bananas.

'17 September: Then I went to build a church for the Pygmies that I named the J. J. Willis church.

'I went further into the forest to a part called Apatanehene and there I found some Pygmies who claim to be the elders of the people. Chabo is their chief . . . I spoke to them and told them it was because they were so far away that we first visited the Bambuba. "You, are you not the most important people in all the areas round here!" When they heard that we gave them so much honour they were very pleased and I got an opportunity to preach to them about the Saviour of all the world, Jesus Christ . . . I gave them three teachers. When evening came then the chief offered me his house. I slept along one side and he along the other . . . I went with interpreters. . . . They (the Pygmies) are very cheerful people and love singing. I asked them to climb some of the trees . . . they climbed and walked along the branches like monkeys, we were afraid for them. Some of them have very pleasant faces, but some have a terrible look, many of the women are very hairy on their bodies. May God in His mercy save many of these people.

'19 September: I set off to Geti to take part in a case where some pagans had beaten up some Christians.

'26 September: I again went to the forest with a party of 56 people. I baptized at Kamega, where there was a crowd of 250. They had come from all the churches around—Mboga, Bulei, Kyabagazi, Bukima, Budingiri, Kainama, Bulega.'

Apolo baptized Yohana Lujumba and his wife Malyamu and their child Yakobo. This was a great occasion, as these were the first people to be baptized in the forest, and the chiefs Kamega, Sabuna, and Kabaya had food cooked for all the visitors. Apolo stayed three days with the baptized family and then went on into deeper parts of the forest to find the Pygmies. 'We felt so happy having taught the Pygmies.'

'12 October: We prayed in the new church at Budingiri, there were 109 people.'

There were by now about seventeen new churches, including Bulega, Buguje, and Bulei outside the forest. Apolo visited at least a third of them each month and the principal centres like Bukima, Budingiri, and Kamega more often.

'30 October: We went to the Pygmies under their chief Apabune . . . We taught a group of 50 of them, all were interested.

'At Banditoli we found an encampment of 75 Pygmies, and their chief Kahuru, they were all out hunting, one man and his wife remaining in camp. While we waited for the others to return they built me a house in $1\frac{1}{2}$ hours! When the others returned I told them why I had come. They said they had heard of me. In the morning about 40 of them gathered together and I told them about Jesus.'

Included here are stories told by the teachers of some of Apolo's encounters with the Pygmies. Some have the authentic touch and others illustrate how legend has undoubtedly embellished some of Apolo's exploits.

Nasani tells that when Apolo first came amongst the Pygmies he would sit down in their midst and sing to them. This amused them greatly and they jumped about with pleasure. They were amazed that an old man (age is venerated), with grey hair and beard, should sit down among them and sing to them in an unknown tongue.

They would all gather round to shake his hand. After this, friendliness was established and he would talk to them through an interpreter.

Salt was one of the commodities most valued by the Pygmies and a gift of salt was a well-known means of winning their friendship. It is said that Apolo very often took salt with him to encourage the Pygmies (this would be the coarse crystalline salt from Lake Katwe in Toro), but as Nasani relates: 'The Pygmies always expected gifts, but never gave any! They asked Apolo for his kanzu and he gave it to be cut into loincloths. They liked to ask to borrow, but had no idea of returning the loan; if you asked for a thing back there would be a dreadful row! So Apolo warned his people never to lend, but to give if they felt inclined. Apolo had great patience with the Pygmies and their ways and customs. He loved them and they knew he loved them and therefore he could manage them, but they knew the teachers did not care for them, the Banyamboga despised them.'

On another occasion the teachers were very nervous when Apolo slept with the Pygmy chief in his hut. 'They kept awake all night keeping guard, lest evil befall. The next day the Pygmies demanded Apolo's bedclothes, he refused to part with them, but promised to send some cloth when he got back to Mboga. The porters understood the Pygmies to say "Let us kill him"and advised Apolo to get away quickly, Apolo said "No", and beat the drum to call them all together that he might preach to them. This so gained their confidence that they said "We cannot kill this man, the things he says are good." The next night they all slept peacefully and then returned to Mboga. Apolo remembered his promise, and sent them cloth and salt.' It is the custom in Africa to take a present when visiting, but the Pygmies obviously exploited this!

'In another part of the forest some Pygmies were settling a dispute by fighting. As Apolo's party approached the encampment and heard the fighting, his terrified teachers held back, but Apolo walked on into the centre of the village. This diversion immediately stopped the fighting; many of the Pygmies were injured by the poisoned arrows, but they have an antidote.'

Peradarsi Kahwa tells how Apolo was teaching the Pygmies one day when a message was received saying that a woman gathering firewood had been caught and crushed to death by a python. Whereupon the chief accused Apolo of bringing this misfortune upon them and told him to leave at once. 'Apolo answered nothing, but got up quickly to go away with his people, and the chief took his bow and arrow to kill Apolo. He shot at him, but the arrow went through his hat, which fell off, thus he was not injured. He knelt down with his teachers to give thanks to God, saying to them "Do not fear this chief, let us not run away." He went back undeterred and no danger came to him. When he died the Pygmies wept much for him.'

Yusufu Limenya tells how Apolo entered into the spirit of the Pygmy enjoyment of song and dance, and taught them to sing some of the simple hymns in Kiswahili. He liked to sit with them round their fires at night. He tells how Apolo took them into his tent (he was later given one by Dr Schofield) and would like to take the children on his knee.

Tomasi tells how they were caught by a heavy rainstorm in one of the Pygmy villages and 'they all huddled into one of the huts, and of course the rain poured through, making Tomasi and the other teachers very miserable. Apolo did not mind at all, saying, "What harm can a little rain do, when we are having such a grand opportunity for fellowship and teaching?" '

The teachers left with the Pygmies did not always have an easy time. Yusufu Limenya, a Mukonjo, who could communicate with the Pygmies, was for many years stationed at Kainama and attempted to stay with the Pygmies in their encampments; he had to trade salt for his food, and when the salt ran out they would no longer feed him. However, undeterred he hunted rats in some deserted Bambuba huts, and with a sufficiently large 'bag' he was welcomed back and fed for three days! He also attempted to go hunting with his Pygmy friends, but these small people got through places he could not manage without 'breaking his back'. They hunt from early morning to late at night, and Yusufu found he could not keep up with such a strenuous life.

Response of the forest churches

Apolo's diary for 1925 is a similar record of ceaseless activity, visiting Pygmy camps and supervising the forest churches: 'I taught them about keeping their churches clean and in good repair. . . .' A severe drought caused famine in the forest, the people were reduced to eating the stems of banana trees. Apolo shared their miserable food.

In June he walked to Toro for the church council. In July he was back in the forest. The Bishop visited Mboga in August. 'I took the Bishop into the forest together with the Bishop's wife . . .' Mrs Willis describes their arrival at Mboga. 'We were met by a crowd of enthusiastic little boys lined up on each side of the path . . . with bunches of flowers tied on the end of long wands, and as we reached their ranks, they gave three resounding cheers for the Bishop. It was too dark to see the faces of the men, women and children who greeted us warmly, as we proceeded down an avenue of trees, past the church, to a little round rest house built by Apolo for travellers. When we entered we found clean white matting on the floor, camp chairs round the table, on which was a jar of flowers, and some photos of missionaries, and a religious picture hanging on the wall. There was an air of neatness and orderliness pervading it all which we found afterwards was one of the characteristics of Apolo. He of course was there to meet us, and sat and chatted, asking us how we had fared upon our journey from Toro, while our tents were being pitched on the ground outside the rest house. Next morning, being Sunday, we proceeded down the avenue of pretty flowering trees to the church for the Confirmation Service. The people were all assembled and there was a great atmosphere of reverence and attention throughout the Confirmation Service, when forty-six were confirmed, twenty-seven men and nineteen women. The son (Thomas Opedi) of old chief Paulo (who had begun by ill treating Apolo and ended by loving him dearly) was also being confirmed with his wife. They all came to tea with us afterwards. Paulo had a particularly nice face. . . . Apolo's face was beaming as it usually does, radiating goodness. He was telling us how he taught the people to work with their hands. I asked him if he did that first of all, or whether he taught them to read first. He said "First of all, I teach them religion and how to read, I nearly broke myself teaching that old man to read" pointing to Paulo, who quite enjoyed the joke, "and then" he said, "I teach them to make roads and plant trees, and to build houses". Everything we saw at Mboga is of course the result of Apolo's work.'

She also mentions the church at Bulei 'which was built on the Model of Mboga, also with an avenue of trees leading to it'. Before leaving Mboga they inspected the handwork at the school, 'Mats and baskets of really beautiful workmanship, taught them by Apolo. The reading and singing of Ruben's boys was especially good. . . . We also saw the work done by the girls, then there were sports, and meetings for the teachers, and a visit to Apolo's own house, which was of interest. His own little bedroom, like a monk's cell, was as neat as an officer's cabin in the Royal Navy. Here Apolo spends from two to four every morning in reading and prayer. . . .'

For the remaining months of the year Apolo is in and out of the forest. 'I pulled down the old church at Kainama and brought it to Makanga. . . . We put on the rafters. . . . We had our prayers in that new church with just the framework around . . . we finished cutting the grass. . . . Everywhere I went and passed along I found people waiting for me by the roadside. When we reached the church I prayed with them and preached to them the Gospel of Jesus.'

'1 December: On these journeys into the forest the Lord indeed has been working wonderfully. It is wonderful to see the heathen turning to God, and helping to cut poles and working with their hands and preparing grass for the church of God. We were surprised at the heathen giving us food that we did not need to buy and calling us friends, the men and the women. These things did indeed cause us to know the blessing of God.'[10]

NOTES

[1] Colin M. Turnbull, *The Forest People* (1961). This fascinating study of the Pygmies of the Ituri forest is by a man who spoke their language and lived with a group for three years. It is interesting to note that the Pygmies, though so distinct as a race, have lost all but the slightest traces of their own language, and have adopted the language of the tribe with whom they associate.

[2] Told by Nasani Kabarole.

[3] E. H. Winter in his monograph on the Baamba alludes to the presence of a group of cannibal witches in each village. Such a group preys upon the members of its own village and reciprocates hospitality tendered by similar groups in other villages. E. H. Winter, *Bwamba*, pp. 150-1.

[4] The religious beliefs of these tribes are centred in the presence of a host of supernatural spirits, those of the ancestors and other entities connected with natural phenomena such as the sun and moon, fire and storms, and countless others; new ones seem to be constantly invented. (Winter, *op. cit.*, p. 111.) An involved ritual to propitiate these spirits or to gain their favour for various exploits is a constant preoccupation. Small spirit-houses are to be seen in the environs of the village or along nearby paths. Witchcraft is rife among these people and an ever present source of trouble.

[5] 'A Fragment from Apolo', *Uganda Church Review*, July 1931, pp. 89-90.

[6] In the foreword to A. B. Lloyd's book *Apolo of the Pygmy Forest*, Bishop Willis pays a warm tribute. 'Apolo, or, to give him his proper title, Canon Apolo (Apollos) Kivebulaya . . . is one of the outstanding personalities of the Uganda Church. With no great natural ability, and with a minimum of education, he has made his way to the front rank of the Baganda clergy by sheer force of character. When, two years ago, he was selected to hold one of the two canonries reserved for African clergy, the way in which the appointment was welcomed by African and European alike was evidence of the affectionate regard in which he is held by all who know him. Simple-minded and single-hearted, without ambition and without fear, he is a man absolutely devoted to one thing.'

[7] Canon H. Bowers, 'The Village Evangelist', *Uganda Church Review*, June 1932, p. 54.

[8] That there was a 'fine new church' at Mboga, was noted in the *Uganda Church Review*, January 1926, p. 11.

[9] J. Gorju, *Entre le Victoria, l'Albert et l'Edouard* (1920), pp. 56-57. J. H. M. Beattie 'Nyoro Personal Names', *Uganda Journal*, vol. 21 (1957), p. 99.

[10] A note in the *Uganda Church Review*, April 1926, p. 42 can be included here. 'The work in Eastern Congo, under Canon Apolo Kivebulaya has

probably extended as far as it is wise beyond Mboga. Apolo is certainly a remarkable personality, and his influence both with natives and Europeans, seems to be steadily growing. The work is carried out in the face of considerable difficulties, but it is one of the brightest spots in our Mission, and a striking evidence of what a native Christian working single-handed can do.'

II

THE FAITHFUL SHEPHERD

<hr>

Apolo's prayer

THIS prayer, written in Luganda, was found after his death on 30 May 1933, at the back of his small pocket diary for that year.

> O God our Father,
> And His Son Jesus Christ,
> And the Holy Spirit,
> May you give me a blessing while in this world,
> While you lead me through the forests,
> Through the lakes and the mountains,
> So that I may do your work among your people,
> Grant that I may be loved by you,
> And by your people. Amen.

Closing Years 1926–32

The records for the years 1926–30 are scanty. In 1926 Apolo spent most of his time travelling in Toro, and we know that he was Rural Dean for Toro in 1927 during the absence of Rev. W. S. R. Russell.

In March 1926 he mentions that he was translating a book for the Pygmies. This was probably the 'pamphlet in Lumbuti' mentioned by Lloyd, which Apolo sent him to be printed.[1] It probably contained the Lord's prayer, Commandments and hymns. At the same time Apolo had got a forest teacher called Yoasi

Otubo to begin a translation of St Mark's Gospel into Rumbuba.[2]
It appears that it was completed by the time Apolo died in 1933.[3]

Apolo visited Mboga on three occasions during 1926. On the
first visit he went to Kamega in the forest, accompanied by sixty-
four of the Mboga Christians, to baptize three more of the forest
people. On the second forest journey he was recalled to Mboga.
'Our beloved Vikitoliya, the mother of Paulo Tabaro has died. I
returned to bury her. I hope she will be found in the gathering
in Heaven'.

The bereaved Mukama wrote the following letter to Apolo
after he had returned to Toro. It appears that Paulo Tabaro, who
had been reinstated by the Belgians in 1925, was taking his duties
seriously.

Boga
30 August 1926

The head of the region (spiritually), Rev. A. Kivebulaya.
    I ask you to pray four things for me.

1. That God may strengthen my heart during this difficult time,
   for I have lost my dear mother Vikitoliya. If God could stop the
   worries I am getting these days it would be a great relief to me.
2. That God may give me wisdom as he has given to you my
   father to do everything in great wisdom.
3. That I may trust in Him and he may look after all my doing in
   return.
4. That He may make me grow up and lead his sheep in a right
   way, as I look after them. That He may go with me in all my
   leadership among His people, so that I may be a good leader of
   the country and make it able to develop. May the Lord be my
   guide in everything, and may his blessings always go with me.

I am, Omukama Paulo Tabaro

Dear Sir, do not forget to pray these things for me your servant.

In 1927 Apolo was elected a Vice-President of the Church
Missionary Society, and in June he attended the C.M.S. Jubilee
celebrations at Kampala, where Miss Baring-Gould remembers
meeting him and congratulating him on his election. 'He said

he knew that now he was a member of the great C.M.S. council and felt very honoured, his dear old face was shining with the light of God, a real "aura". I felt it, I felt like kneeling down and asking him for his blessing.'⁴

Miss Baring-Gould tells how delegates were gathered at Kampala from all the far corners of the Protectorate. 'They had flocked in from Teso and Lango, from Toro and Bunyoro, from Ankole and Kigezi, from Busoga and Bukedi. Variety in feature and language, variety in intellectual powers and attainments, some whose ancestors were deadly foes now friends; "all one in Jesus Christ". There to give thanks and mindful of the past fifty years'.⁵ At the celebrations 'the story was told of the painful and laborious sowing of the seed in 1877 until 1890, when harvesting began, and the Church grew, was built up and consolidated in the Faith. The story was told of the Missionary work of the Church, a wonderful and inspiring story . . . how that one Church with about 200 members on the hill at Namirembe in 1890 had now become 2,000 Churches with nearly 185,000 baptized members—a great Church, self-supporting as regards its own native organization, self-governing and self-extending'.⁶

On 30 June, the day began with the burial of Alexander Mackay's remains, lately brought from Usambiro, at the south of Lake Victoria, and laid to rest beside the great brick cathedral, its walls now gilded by the morning sun. Beside his grave stood those who knew him, 'his boys', and the African clergy, the Bishops of Uganda and the Upper Nile, of Nyasaland, Mombasa, Zanzibar and Masasi, notables and chiefs and people from all over Uganda.

'On the coffin was laid one of the few remaining copies of Mackay's great gift to the Uganda Church, the Gospel of St Matthew in Luganda, printed in 1887 and sewn together in a loose cover of barkcloth . . . In this manner Mackay came home'.⁷

A great thanksgiving service in the cathedral followed, a beautiful Bible was presented by the British and Foreign Bible Society, which was then read by Canon Apolo (Heb. 11.32–12.2), after which a memorial tablet to Bishop Hannington was unveiled in the Hannington chapel.

On the following Saturday there was a Schools' rally, sports and a concert, at which Apolo gave an address. He indeed had seen changes in these fifty years.

In 1928 Apolo was back at Mboga, visiting the forest churches, repairing and rebuilding where fire and neglect had destroyed.

It may have been during the years 1928–30 that the notorious cannibal, Bantumangia, came to be converted and baptized as a Christian.

Yusufu and Nasani described him as the leader of a group of sorcerers within the Bahuku tribe. 'They made a feast and shared it round. One of his customs was to cut off some small bone from each of his victims, and wrapping it in barkcloth, would hang it with all the others on a string round his neck, the idea being that these relics would keep him safe from the vengeance of the spirits of his victims'.

Yusufu explained that the Bahuku as a tribe practised cannibalism in time of war, 'but one individual, especially an oldish man, would get a great taste for human flesh. He would lead a group of like-minded people who would deliberately hunt their victims. A cannibal hunt was announced by a special kind of drumming.'[8] Yusufu continues—'This cannibal had a grandson who had been taught and was baptized Yosiya. Yosiya told his grandfather the gospel story. The cannibal said "Tell the teacher to come here, that I may believe". Yosiya came to Yusufu and asked him to go to his grandfather out there in the forest. Yusufu went with him to the cannibal's hut. They first sat down to a meal outside and when night came he took Yusufu into his hut, the grandson sleeping elsewhere. In the middle of the hut was a fire. Yusufu began talking to him, saying, "What are these bad things that you have been doing?" "We have been eating Pygmies," answered the cannibal. "Pygmy meat is much better than other meat, it is as savoury as pork".' (One may feel doubtful about this statement. The Pygmies were too quick and astute to be easily caught by the Buhuku. However, the fact that in these parts they associated with the Bambuba may indicate that they were preyed upon by the Bahuku.)

Yusufu spent a nervous night in the cannibal's hut; he saw some joints of meat hung up in smoke, which he recognized as wild pig. He saw these joints and knew that they were not human meat, only he feared that during the night he might be attacked and stored for a meal. However, he recovered his courage and explained the Gospel to Bantumangia. The cannibal then wanted to be baptized. Yusufu said, 'I cannot baptize you, but there is a man, Apolo Kivebulaya, who will baptize you when he comes round this way again.' Yusufu also explained that he would need to be instructed before being baptized. 'You live a very long way off and I cannot come all this way to teach you.' The cannibal wished to be baptized quickly, so Yusufu suggested he should come to Kainama for a week's instruction every fortnight. The man still feared very much to agree with this plan, because on his way to and fro he would have to pass through enemy territory, but because of his great desire to be baptized he was willing to take the risk. The instructions continued in this way for three months. Yusufu taught him alone, as the rest of the baptismal class consisted of young people. The time came for Apolo to visit them and Yusufu spoke to the man about his 'necklace' of gruesome relics, telling him to take it off, but he still feared to do this; however, he promised to take it off on the day of his baptism.

Nasani tells how, on the day he was to be baptized at Bwakadi, 'there he was in church, with the other candidates, decked out in his charms, yet hoping to be baptized with the rest. No one could believe he really wanted to be baptized, he was so greatly feared'.

Apolo questioned him carefully and they tell how the cannibal was afraid to take off this powerful necklace himself, so Nasani was told to take it off, which he did, he admits, not without certain apprehension. 'The people around expected to see Nasani and Apolo die immediately, so great was the power of those charms.

'They then returned to the church for the baptismal service, and in his sermon Apolo preached about the uselessness of these things, the power of Christ was greater than all these . . . The tall old man was baptized and very happy, he took the name of Apolo! He publicly destroyed his cooking pots and sorcerer's paraphernalia, also the spirit hut where he made his offerings.

'This man went on steadily in the Christian life until he died. Yusufu taught him hymns in his own tongue. He preached to his neighbours and they listened because his life was so obviously changed. He came to live near the church at Intergessa, and is buried there.'

There is a small C.M.S. diary of Apolo's for 1931 which gives a clearer idea of his day-to-day activities at Mboga and his visits to the forest. He was by now an old man of 67; none the less he seldom took a day off. The entries show that he followed a weekly routine, daily teaching the 'teachers'; these would be older boys and girls who would in turn teach the younger ones; the more able were sent to the forest. It is also told that those stationed in the forest were recalled at intervals for further training.

There was also a growing number of candidates to be prepared for confirmation. A special prayer meeting was held in the church every Friday. Saturdays were spent giving out medicines (supplied by the C.M.S. doctor in Toro) and visiting the sick and the Christians in their homes, unless varied by a wedding ceremony or church council. On Sundays there would be a celebration of Holy Communion and a service with sermon.

Reading between the lines of these entries we can also see a multitude of other concerns which filled his days, the general supervision and discipline of the school and the young people who lived with him, his unfailing hospitality. It is said he taught the women who did the cooking for his household to bake altar bread in a kerosene tin over an open fire, and he made church wine himself from banana juice when the supply from Toro was finished. The church and school and their surroundings had to be kept tidy and clean. He was very particular about the cleanliness of the church vestments and his own clothes. A large charcoal iron was installed in his house. He was also responsible for the church moneys. A simple account appears in his diary for 1929.

'1. The gifts for December and the Christmas collection was given to the teachers, the rest went to the bag of the church of Mboga.

'2. Sunday collections go to help in building the teachers' houses. The rest is put in the bag of Mboga.

'3. Money from selling books goes to feed the schoolchildren who come from all over the place and spend four years here. Also this money helps to get them clothes.

'4. Money sent by our friends in England and in Buganda is given to the teachers.

'5. Money sent from Kampala (his own pay?) also goes to the teachers.

'6. Some of the money which comes from our friends goes to help feed those who are teaching the Pygmies.'

Lloyd wrote, 'His knowledge . . . of keeping accounts was primitive indeed; in fact, he once told me he only kept two bags for his money. Into one of these he emptied all the collections and called it the "Teachers' Bag", and into the other went school fees and subscriptions and gifts used entirely for school work. When either of these bags was getting empty he just asked the Christians to replenish them.'[9]

Apolo's visiting in the forest did not slacken with his increasing age. He was by now visiting fourteen places in the forest regularly, at least five or six of them each month, and holding confirmation classes at Kainama and Makanga in preparation for the Bishop's visit in February, when he confirmed these people in the forest. The usual delightful welcome was prepared for the Bishop's visit, with the schoolchildren lining the road, holding long reeds with brightly coloured flowers on the ends, singing a song of welcome. 'Apolo with his beaming smile and joyous welcome' led the whole cavalcade into the church singing a joyful hymn.[10]

The Bishop remarked that the forest churches were often wonderfully well built and that the primitive, unclothed congregations, still in the earliest stages of evangelization, had yet an unmistakable sense of reverence and reality. Evidently singing was made to play a large part in the work of evangelization, simple hymns being sung over and over again with great gusto.

Of Apolo himself, the Bishop wrote that clearly the whole strength of the work lay in him. He was indeed master in his strangely assorted household of many people, who not only obeyed but loved and implicitly trusted him. He shared their life and gave himself to them. But besides this more obvious reason for success, he was a man of prayer. It had been his practice for more than twenty years to set aside time for private prayer at night when others were asleep. 'The unfailing cheerfulness, the practical common sense, the direct telling speech, the steady perseverance year after year, all have their roots here. And something at least of his spirit has entered into his people . . .'[11]

Apolo wrote to Bishop Willis soon after he left them telling how greatly his visit had stimulated the people. 'The Pygmies of their own accord sent in a deputation to Mboga from Makanga to thank me especially for calling them to see such a number of visitors. They said, "How good God is to join us together with the Europeans. We have never before seen so many Europeans together (five!) and they greeted us with faces that did not despise us".'[12]

In his letter to the *Uganda Church Review* Apolo again refers to this visit. 'It was a wonder when the Bishop confirmed 115 people in the forest. After the Bishop left, messengers came to me from the forest from places four days' journey through the forest. They saw those people whom the Bishop had confirmed and they sent messengers to ask for teachers. I am glad I have been able to give them teachers. I am not going to tire you or take up the space of other writers. The work in the Congo excels in strength and joy. I do not sit in the house, but I travel in the forest. He who appeared to me has given me grace in difficult languages. My teachers have overcome them. The Bishop preached in every tongue through interpreters. I have much strength to finish the work which He who appeared to me gave me to do until death.'[13]

In May 1931 Apolo records the death of the Mukama Paulo Tabaro, who shot himself with a gun while suffering from mental illness. On 16 May 'we buried Paulo Tabaro . . . I went to visit the bereaved of the Mukama . . . we inherited a chair from Paulo Tabaro. His son Thomas Opedi Byensi Tabaro became the new Mukama, and he came and prayed with us in the church.'

The diary for the rest of 1931 is a similar record of arduous work. There is no record for 1932, but it is not likely that it varied greatly from the previous year, except that an increasing tiredness made the work heavier. Apolo's teachers tell how, on their tramps into the forest the old priest complained of the cold and wet, and his boys had to push him up all the hills.

Nasani tells that during this year Apolo baptized two groups of Pygmies (the first Pygmies to be baptized in the forest). These two groups had settled near Makanga, he had taken great trouble to instruct them. 'He baptized these groups, in one all the men were named Abraham and all the women Sarah! In the other he named all the men Matthew and the women Mary! These groups did not scatter until after Apolo died and so they could be taught. They go around in a kind of circuit every three years or so, but if anyone dies the group immediately moves on.'

On his last journey into the forest he spent much time questioning those preparing for baptism, hoping to come back and baptize them later.

Departure

A small C.M.S. pocket book for 1933 is extant and has short entries for the remaining months of Apolo's life.[14]

In January the entries are as usual. He is teaching his classes, visiting the sick and holding church services, marrying and burying his people. It is clear that his health was failing and he felt a visit to a doctor was necessary. On 24 February he went over to Toro. He was probably carried in a hammock slung on a pole, but when he got to Toro he still had enough energy to visit Nyakasura for discussions, and to give an address to a teachers' class. On the 30th he was taken to Kampala by car, where at Mengo Hospital Sir Albert Cook examined him and found that his heart was failing. He ordered three months' rest, but Apolo knew he was going to die and was determined to get back to Mboga to die among 'his people', so they let him go. His friend Aberi Balya was with him and they got a lift back by car to Kabarole. Aberi Balya continues the story, 'He stayed in his house at Kabarole, he was not at all well, his legs began to swell. He said to us, "Carry me and take me back to Mboga." I said to him, "You are not going back to Mboga, we want you to stay here, and when you die we will bury you by the church here, we want your grave to be with us here." He said, "If you don't return me to Mboga, you will bury me badly."

'Then Russell and I took counsel together and we decided to send him back to Mboga. People carried him, and he bade farewell to Toro, to the people who came to say goodbye to him, with great joy . . . about 50 Christians from Mboga were waiting for him at the Semliki to take over from the Toro carriers.[15] When he arrived back at Mboga he got steadily worse. On 22 May I received a telephone message from Mboga (for some years a single telephone wire connected Irumu, Mboga and Fort Portal) that Apolo was dying. I went to see the Provincial Commissioner to ask permission to go to Mboga. I had to pay 14 shillings and 50 cents for a wire to get permission. They granted me permission quickly. I set out on the 23 May and got there on the 25th. I found him very ill and very swollen. He was very pleased to see me. He drew me down to himself as he lay and greeted me with such a joyful embrace. His heart was not thinking about death, but about the work. He said, "In the morning you will give Holy Communion to the teachers, and afterwards you will go into the forest and baptize those people whom I examined, whom I have not been able to baptize because of my illness." I said to him, "But I cannot, my feet are already cut and pricked with thorns from the journey to Mboga, anyway I have come to bury you." He said nothing, but I could see he was not pleased. Then I told him that Omwami Yosiya Sewali, the *Katikiro* of Toro, had sent him a bolt of cloth to bury him in. He said to me, "In the morning I will send it to the teachers in the forest." I was surprised. Other things I had to say I refrained from saying.

'On 26 May the teachers came in for Holy Communion, it was an important day, Apolo was worse. The Rev. Russell and his wife arrived on the 27 May; he had come from Ankole where he had been on a tour of the Deanery. Apolo was very pleased to see them.

'On Sunday the 28th we took the bread and wine and gave Apolo Holy Communion as he lay on his bed. We bade farewell to him with the sacrament of the body and blood of Jesus his Lord, for whom he had worked for 38 years, working for Him whom he dearly loved, even until death. He loved Him above anything on this earth. He was very happy indeed . . . I was watching with him in his house, others came too. In the morning I prayed and talked with him about all kinds of things, I asked his thoughts about a lot of things, about the work and who should carry on his work and he answered "Tomasi Ndahura, Nasani Kabarole, Yosiya Kaburwa, Yusufu Limenya, they will be able to help the church in Mboga, I have trained them." I asked him if he had any money in the bank, he said "I have not even one shilling in the bank." I asked him if he had any debts, he said, "There are no debts, except some shillings of Tomasi Ndahura's, which he gave to me and put in the fund for paying the church teachers in the forest, 250 shillings. Sell my table and chairs and kettle and anything else to pay these shillings." He then told me he had two cows at Butiti. "Leave them," he said, "to the church at Mboga. There is nothing else left," and truly there was just nothing else, anything he had had he had already given away. He did not die like other people, who have many possessions, anything he ever possessed he used in the service of God. He ate little and wore little and had few bedclothes, he had neither wife nor child, so he was able to please himself and do what he liked, knowing that when he died he had no one dependent upon him. He knew that God had given him many Christians and they were his children.

'I found as I talked with him that he had been preparing for some time to leave this earth, he said "Let me go, to find those children of mine who have gone before me into Heaven, to be with my Lord, whom I have served from my youth to my old age." Two things he asked before he died, first that there should be no wailing for him and secondly he wished to be buried with his head towards the forest (it is custom to bury a man with his head towards his home) "to signify that I am still going towards the forest to preach the gospel, even now my spirit is towards my work". He spoke in faith and hope. At that time he was very ill . . . and swollen from his feet to his head and he breathed with great difficulty, but all the time he was full of joy and peace, without fear or worry. He was a marvellous witness to all. To those who came to visit him, he led them in sickness as he had led them in health, and he led them too in death. To us the workers, he was a great example in life and in death—as St Paul worked so did Apolo, both were bond servants. I finished talking with Apolo on 29th, that was the last time I spoke with him. On the 30 May at 2.45 p.m. Canon Apolo Kivebulaya died. He left this world to go to another which has no poverty or sorrow. He rested with a quiet happy face as if asleep. I was there, together with Damari Ngaju, a woman who was the first to be baptized at Mboga . . . So Apolo fell asleep in the midst of his people . . . I sent for Canon and Mrs Russell. They came and found him gone. We knelt and thanked God for all the good things He had enabled Apolo to do. Then they went away, I and some others remained to prepare his body for the burying, we placed it in a coffin which we had brought from Toro, the gift of the Mukama George Rukidi. Then some of the Belgians came to pay their respects. They were indeed all very sorry, for they had great respect for him and the work he had done in their country. They helped us a lot.

'On the 31st May at 10 a.m. we buried Canon Apolo, we buried him near the church at Mboga. . . .'

Canon Russell records: 'Early in the morning I had gone down to the church to see that all was in readiness for the service. I found the church beautifully decorated with flowers as for a festival. What did it mean? It was a spontaneous act of the Christians themselves. They knew how Apolo had loved flowers, but it had also I think a deeper significance. They were deep in grief because they had lost their beloved leader, but this act of theirs was also an attempt to express their faith in a greater fact, that he had passed into a higher life and service.'[16]

Aberi Balya tells how he himself stayed on, to do many things. 'From 1 to 4 June I spent in the forest, baptizing many people, and helping to strengthen them, they were very pleased to hear that I was a friend of Apolo's. In the forest I was surprised to see so many excellent churches with clean well-kept flower beds and compounds. Neat furnishings in the church, all in such good order, the schools also, and so many attending them. Many Pygmies came to see me, and with tears told me how great a friend Apolo had been to them. I visited fourteen churches and baptized many people, children and adults. I also administered Holy Communion to many who had been without owing to Apolo's illness.'

Apolo had urged the C.M.S. to send a European missionary to take over the expanding work at Mboga. Although he hoped that the teachers he had nominated would go forward to be trained for ordination, he himself knew the need for a trained and educated missionary to consolidate the work that he had pioneered.

NOTES

[1] Letter from Lloyd to Apolo, London, 30 June 1926. There is no language known as Lumbuti. The Pygmies in these parts spoke Rumbuba.

[2] At Lloyd's suggestion; Lloyd to Apolo, London 25 November 1925. These letters were pasted into Apolo's diary.

[3] It was sent to the British and Foreign Bible Society, whose translations secretary prepared a tentative grammar and dictionary and a typescript of the translation of St Mark. These were later sent to Mboga with a view to their being checked. (Correspondence between Mrs F. E. Ridsdale and the Translation Department of the British and Foreign Bible Society, 1950.)

[4] Extract from Miss E. M. E. Baring-Gould's journal.

[5] E. M. E. Baring-Gould, 'Jubilee Memories', *Uganda Church Review*, December 1927, p. 130.

[6] Archdeacon Blackledge, 'Jubilee Missions in Uganda', *Uganda Church Review*, July 1927, p. 73.

[7] Miss Warburton, 'The Home Coming of Alexander Mackay', *Uganda Church Review*, December 1927, p. 119.

[8] This is described by J. T. Muirhead, 'The *dingwinti* drum is made from a tree trunk hollowed out right through. Over one end a brayed skin is stretched and fastened with wooden nails. The other end is left open, a hole is made in the centre of the skin and a stick about the thickness of your finger put through this, which has a knob on one end to prevent its being pulled through the head of the drum when played.

'The drummer, sitting on the ground, holds the drum between his legs with its head on the opposite side to him. He then wets his fingers with water and pulls the stick inside the drum towards him. After he has got a good tension on it he lets it slip through his fingers. This sets up a vibration of the skin which can be regulated from a very loud noise to a very slight . . .

and is made as weird as possible, often like moaning. This drum is played only by the witch-doctor and means death and torture to someone, or perhaps a lot of them. When it is played the people sit about in great dread and seem to be mesmerized, for no one at the time knows whose doom it may be that is rubbed out on that weird instrument.' J. T. Muirhead, *Ivory Poaching and Cannibals in Africa* (1933), pp. 53–54.

[9] A. B. Lloyd, 'Canon Apolo', *Church Assembly News*.

[10] Rev. W. S. R. Russell, 'Diary of a Missionary Tour to Mboga'.

[11] J. J. Uganda (Bishop Willis), 'Mboga', *The Church Overseas*, January 1932, pp. 56–58.

[12] *The Church Overseas*, January 1932, p. 59.

[13] 'A Fragment from Apolo', *Uganda Church Review*, July 1931, pp. 89–90.

[14] C.M.S. Archives.

[15] Letter from Apolo to Russell, Mboga, 27 April 1933.

[16] W. S. R. Russell, 'The Passing of Apolo', in *Apolo the Pathfinder*, p. 66.

Part Three

EPILOGUE

12

A PORTRAIT

The fruit of the Spirit

IN a short film taken of Apolo some years before his death we
see him walking down the avenue of trees at Mboga; on either
side are the schoolchildren waving reeds with bunches of flowers to
welcome a party of missionaries. Apolo is a small, slightly built man
with a gentle unobtrusive manner. Later he somewhat shyly sub-
mits to being photographed by himself seated at a table.[1]

It is difficult to assess the character of Apolo at this distance, the
more so because of the imposing list of Christian virtues attached
to his memory. The contemporary world is not satisfied until a
man has been stripped, and his inner life prised open to reveal
hidden weaknesses. Even if this were possible in Apolo's case there
would be no point in doing so. Before God human nature at its best
is weak and imperfect, but God uses this weak material to accom-
plish his holy work in the world. The evidence from the lives of the
saints is sufficient to prove the truth of Galatians 5.22-23.[2] The
'harvest of the Spirit' was manifest in Apolo, most notably the joy
that shone from him. He was fearless in the face of evil. He did not
compromise his standards, either with the demands of men or the
traditional practices and beliefs of his background. There was a
wholeness about him, an inner and outer balance that marked him
as 'a man of God'.

Apolo's Christianity was a refreshment to others. The Rev.
W. S. R. Russell said of him: 'One felt a better man for having been
with Apolo, his sense of joy was contagious. He was always Apolo,

153

completely unselfconscious and completely natural. He could not be spoilt or patronized. He had no sense of racial differences and was completely at ease with all kinds and conditions of men . . . We call him a great man. He himself would hardly understand our use of the term, because he possessed the first necessity of greatness —a true humility of spirit.'

His simplicity perhaps meant he was more without faults than a temperamental and complex nature would have been. Nowhere is a word raised against him. His liking for nice clothes is an endearing trait and his occasional outbursts of anger against those who were lazy or insolent are hardly to be censured.[3]

It is perhaps as the shepherd of his flock that we shall best remember him. He was an earthly father whose wisdom and understanding of men and concern for them made belief in a Heavenly Father a possibility for them. He loved all the strangely assorted people God called him to care for, and they loved him in return. An assiduous visitor to the Christians in their homes and a tireless traveller to the scattered churches in his pastorate, he seldom rested, nor is there any record of his taking a proper holiday in all the years of his ministry. Tireless and patient in reclaiming those who had 'gone back', he never gave up because a task was difficult. His sense of fun won him access to children and the shy forest Pygmies, who wept for him when he died.

As an evangelist his zeal for winning souls is described as a fire within him; he never missed an opportunity to preach Christ. 'The Gospel is for all men,' he said, and there were none too lowly for his attention.

As a priest, worship meant a very great deal to him. His churches were noted for their order and his efforts to make them fitting and beautiful. His preaching was simple, homely and direct, but he could also be fierce and stern in denouncing evil; yet he was a priest with a healing touch and on his last visit to Kampala he pleaded with great fervour for reconciliation between the black and white races, who both had a place in God's plan for Africa.

He died as he had lived, in happy and peaceful trust in God. His last thoughts were towards his children—those he was leaving behind and those he hoped to find in eternity.

Some memories of Apolo

The following selections from both written accounts and conversations may furnish some idea of the qualities of Apolo's life that were especially noted by the people who knew and loved him.

Patience and love

'Apolo did not distinguish between people . . . He slept in their homes and ate with them, he was found in their gardens preaching to them the gospel . . . he worked with them, he despised no one, he was patient with everyone, it was his way, until a man became a Christian . . .'[5]

'He showed love especially to children. As he walked along, they ran beside him, and he would put his hands on their heads in blessing, wherever he went, they would join him.'[6]

'If he had to rebuke his teachers, it was done privately and not in public.'[6]

'All were brought into his house, including the naked forest tribes and the sick . . . He was a great visitor . . . If he were spoken to rudely he would be silent . . . Although he was held in such great awe, he did not sit in judgement, but would talk to sinners in love and seek to help them . . .'[8]

Humility and power

'Apolo was not a person who liked to receive honour and glory, or to work to gain position and promotion. He did not bother about things like that . . . Sometimes he allowed the younger ones to be promoted over him. One day in the church council, a parson was to be sent to the small place where I had been teaching. It was vacant as I was being sent to Namirembe for further study. This young parson refused to go, he wanted to remain in the more important place, where he was. Immediately Apolo asked if he might go instead, and he went and did a great work in that place . . . People who are like that are very few.'[5]

'Apolo's personality was a power no one would interfere with, a rare power that set him apart as a true man of God, of whom no one could think evil; all the tribes felt this power and called him holy Apolo. With all these people about there was never anything that evil tongues could lay hold of in his life.'[7] 'Wherever he went he spoke, and the people "hung on his words". At the same time they were in awe of him.'[8]

'He was a most able and energetic man, a strong disciplinarian, but not a spoil sport. He would have complete control of a crowd. His judgement was sound. He was utterly fearless in dealing with trouble and he never took sides.'[9]

'One strange example of his power—his garden was not eaten by wild pigs. People were surprised to see their tracks, but none of the food was touched.'[7] Another tells how 'the wild pigs were troubling everyone's garden but his, and the people used to say "You come and stand in our garden and then the pigs won't come!"'[8]

A man of prayer

'This power of God to make him understand was revealed in the times he spent in prayer; all his life a time for prayer and Bible reading was set aside, usually in the early hours of the morning, for the main part of the day was thronged with people.'[7]

'Apolo showed no fear of witchcraft or superstition. The people saw that when he prayed for rain, rain came without the assistance of the rainmakers, who were greatly feared.'[10]

'Apolo was a man of prayer; sometimes he came to stay with us for a rest, it was always he who was up before us and led us in prayer—for the sick, for the posting of teachers, for all the difficulties of the work of which he felt the weight. And when he began to take the gospel into the forest he prayed and covenanted with God to give his whole life to the work in the forest and to be guided by God, without self-pity, without fear of death. This is what he prayed and I heard him—"O God cleanse me, let those things which are before me be pleasing in Thy sight, more than the things which are behind" . . . He always persevered in the prayer that God would open the door of the forest to the word of God. He gave it to him, he went and died there . . .'[5]

Healing power

Tomasi Ndahura tells how Apolo had a gift of healing. 'This was a gift he did not display or use in a general way, but as a special need arose, he had the faith to trust God and act as God directed him. People knew him too well to take advantage of him in these matters . . .'

'Tomasi and his wife came to live in a house at the mission. Their eldest son Bezaleri was taken very ill when he was about two years old and was finally in a semi-conscious state. The women began to wail and cry as they do, and Tomasi called to Apolo, who came across quickly to the child; all the people were wailing as he was near to death; he was clammy and his teeth were clenched. Apolo told the people who crowded the house to stop crying, and picking up the child, carried him out of the house, across to his own room and laid him on his own bed. Apolo forbade the wailing people to come—only Tomasi followed him, but was not allowed to enter. Apolo was alone with the child—he spent time in prayer with him there alone, and then calling Tomasi, he said, "God has helped the child, cheer up, he will be better." Bezaleri sneezed and showed signs of recovery, so Tomasi called the mother and the child opened his eyes and they were very, very surprised. All this took about three hours—but the boy was getting quite well and talking a little. Apolo showed a remarkable confidence all through and had no doubt whatsoever on these occasions.'

'Help was also given to Tomasi over his wife, who was afflicted, like the woman in the gospel, with an issue of blood. They brought the matter to Apolo. He was going on one of his journeys into the forest and said to Tomasi, "Let your wife come with me into the forest". She went with him and eventually they came to a river. Apolo sent the teachers on ahead, he then told the woman to get right into the water. She obeyed him, going right in, and sat there for about an hour. Apolo then told her to get up and come out, and from that time on she was perfectly cured. She continued with him during the two weeks' tour of the forest and came back well.'

Nasani Kabarole also tells one of the healing stories: 'One day when going through the forest Apolo met a woman suffering from severe abdominal pains. She had not been able to eat anything for five days. They asked Apolo if he had any medicine to help this woman. Apolo answered "I have no medicine, but there is something I can do". He then called the heathen people together, to the woman's hut and said, "Let us pray" and he proceeded to pray with faith that this heathen woman should be healed. Apolo then brewed some coffee and gave it to the woman to drink. After two hot cups the pain was relieved. Apolo said "I have not given this woman any medicine, I have prayed to God and He is going to heal her"—and she got well. She joined the baptism class and was eventually baptized and her husband too.'

Poverty and chastity

Apolo enjoyed good clothes and the necessities of life, but possessions had no great claim on him and he parted with them easily. 'Nearly all his pay was given to the teachers. He kept only two coats, two kanzus and a loincloth.'[5]

Apolo had a reputation for chastity. Tomasi tells how 'Apolo was able to have friendships with both sexes. It was a friendship in God. He looked on his people as a father looks upon his children and desired that they should come to know the life of the Spirit and God helped him to divide his life from theirs in that sense. It was a spiritual oversight entirely, a remarkable relationship with one who was master of himself.

'At one time Bishop Willis tried to persuade Apolo to marry, saying "You live in a foreign country, it is better for you to marry", but Apolo refused, saying, "However far you stretch your ears you will never hear anything about me like that". Not even his enemies could find any breath of scandal against him.'[7]

Apolo was noted for his courtesy to women. 'He taught people to respect women and give them their due. "A woman gave birth to Our Lord. A woman was the first to see the risen Christ".'[8]

Courage and peace

The following incidents showing Apolo's quiet courage and whimsical humour were written in his diary, amongst the entries and letters dated 1929–30, and probably refer to the time he was acting Rural Dean of Toro in 1927.

'Daudi Kasagama, the Mukama of Toro, tried to frighten me, saying that as I used to walk in the evening to Bulaya to preach I might be eaten by wild animals. I then answered him saying that as God made me walk to these places, then He would be responsible for my life. These were dangerous times when the animals had become so wild everywhere. They killed so many people in Toro and they were greatly feared, but I did not fear them at all. One day I was walking through the country and I had a small boy with me and we saw two lions, the boy had never seen lions before and said to me "Sir, look at those cows". I then answered that I had already seen them. We passed by them without their moving at all. I then went to preach and on my way back, I found they had already left the place. So God helped me in this.

'Another time when I was walking in Toro (as usual accompanied by a young boy) I went to Mutitiri where the kings of Toro are buried.[4] It became dark while I was there and seeing a hut I asked the woman for a place to spend the night. The woman said, "What silly man is this! You cannot come in here, you will spend the night outside, don't you know that this is the Toro kings' burial place?" I then answered her that I feared the lions might eat the little boy, that he was a Mutoro boy, not a Muganda as I was. Then I begged her to let the boy in as I could stay outside. The woman could not agree, though she knew that lions eat people, even in daylight! All their houses had been fenced around. But when it was 8 o'clock in the night she then let us in. I had been asking for God's help, and he lowered the woman's anger. When I asked her whether she knew God, she told me to stop, otherwise she would send me out of the house. I then saw her bringing me food. I ate and thanked God the Almighty.'

Another story is told of Apolo's good sense in face of danger. 'One day we were coming from the forest and walked unsuspecting into a large herd of elephant, some of the great beasts were standing on the pathway. We retreated and waited behind some trees. Apolo prayed that we might be delivered from the danger; soon the elephants moved off and we walked peacefully to the other side.'[11]

Apolo had no fear of witchcraft. The birth of twins was a pheno-
menon greatly feared by most tribes; complicated taboos and
ceremonies decreed by a witch-doctor were necessary to propitiate
the powers involved, and until these were completed no one would
dare approach the mother and children. 'One day Apolo heard that
one of the baptized Christian women had given birth to twins, so
he went to the hut, and picking up the twins, spoke to the woman
and showed her openly, all the people expecting that someone
would die for this daring behaviour. They soon saw that nothing
happened, and that it saved many expensive offerings. Gradually
these customs broke down, so much so, that even in heathen homes,
they now send for the parson to liberate them and break the
spells'.[10]

Fear is Africa's greatest affliction. The tribute that Apolo had
no fear, that he was always cheerful and unruffled,[12] is notable in a
country where mutual mistrust and suspicion most commonly mar
human relationships.

Teaching and preaching

Apolo's teaching was leavened with good sense—'the gospel is
for the whole man', he used to say.[8] He taught self-discipline in the
matters of order and cleanliness and encouraged the people to
develop their own handicrafts.

Bishop Balya tells how Apolo taught him. 'God gave him great
gifts of learning and understanding and the ability to pass on that
knowledge. He taught me a little geography and told me about
England so vividly you would think he had visited there . . . and
truly he encouraged us to teach ourselves so that we might obtain
food to feed others . . . his steady quiet study of the Bible made
him a rich man in the word in his heart . . . I remember how very
fond Apolo was of teaching about St Paul's journeys; he knew them
all by heart . . . He also had many good ideas about teaching
boys and girls, and what they should be taught that would make
them useful to their nation, and even now in Toro and Mboga we
are reaping the profits.'

'He was at the same time a disciplinarian with the boys, he did not like anyone to say "I cannot do this or that", he would say "go and do it and learn".'[5]

'Apolo always said "If there be difficulties it means that there is plenty of work to be done, for that is the work God has called us to do. Let us put all our effort into it, for where there are no difficulties, there is no work at all!" '[11]

'When questioning candidates for baptism the questions were put in a different form to each one, so that the answers were not just a rote! He was keen to make them learn texts and passages "in their heads" . . . His system of teaching was all question and answer.'[7]

Two illustrations show how Apolo used local proverbs to drive home his teaching—*Okwekwatera kusumera* means 'a man who has a shield and spear rejoices in his strength'. Apolo would say, 'Wherefore his joy? Because he is armed for warfare—so we should clasp Christ to ourselves. He is our shield and defence.'

Another of his favourites was *Alindira kihweyo afumita mukira*— 'He who waits till it goes by—spears the tail!'—'Procrastination is the thief of time!'[13]

'Apolo instructed the girls about Christian marriage, and none would have dreamt of marrying anyone he did not approve of. They were mostly grateful for his care. Those who went against him were not happy. After their marriages he kept in touch with them. He did not approve of mixed marriages and illicit connections with Belgians, producing half-casts for "prestige" and "money". "You will be cursed, no blessing will come." '[8]

The Rev. Asa Byara remembers one of Apolo's sermons. As a young school-teacher in 1931 he confessed his critical attitude towards the uneducated old priest who came one day to address a class of school-teachers and educated chiefs. 'I in my pride wondered, when old Apolo came into the room, how he was going to present his talk and how it was going to be received by such an intelligent group of men. His text was—"How beautiful are the feet of them that preach the gospel of peace, and bring glad tidings of good things" (Rom. 10.15). We were all greatly moved and challenged by his message. It was one of the best sermons I have ever heard.'

Dr Schofield gives an example of Apolo's down-to-earthness in his sermons. 'Like Jesus Himself, his approach to people was through their everyday life and everyday things. Here are some examples I can remember. One day, when our camp was pitched under the Ruwenzori mountains many of our porters were Bakonjo, a tribe who live up on the mountains. I asked Apolo to take our usual evening camp prayers and to speak especially to the Bakonjo. Here is a summary of his approach. "You Bakonjo are very much luckier than we are. You live up there in the mountains and so are nearer to God, who lives up in Heaven. Yes, you are a lot luckier than we are, who live down here. Why, we have to send up to ask you for the best wood for our furniture which grows up in your mountains. Yes, and all the rivers we have, come down from where you live, and so we have to drink the water after you have washed yourselves." You can imagine their shouts of laughter and how they listened to the rest of his message.

'Another time, I asked Apolo to preach at our hospital service. He said that if they went to the witch-doctor when they were ill, they had to take him a cow or a sheep before he would see them, and when they left him they often were no better, and perhaps died. But if they came to the Christian hospital, they got better and then afterwards were asked for a small gift to show their thanks. "Yes," he said, "you do not have to pay a cow before you come, and only a few shillings when you get better, and nothing at all if you die!" More shouts of laughter, but real hanging on to his words as he went on to speak of God's care and love for them.

'Perhaps one other instance is when he was preaching in a big church in Advent, on preparing for Christmas and for the coming of Jesus. He turned to the men (the sexes sit on different sides in the church) and said "We men, we know nothing of it at all, but you women, you know all about what it was like for Mary to have Jesus inside her for nine months", and then he went on to hammer home the need for the expectancy and for the preparation for the coming of the Lord.'

Mrs Schofield remembers his preaching at a children's service.

'He was preaching on St Paul, saying, "you children, you are all baptized in infancy, and you are all free-born into the privilege of Christ, but we older ones, we had to enter like the centurion, and we could say "with a great price obtained I this freedom". Yes, and do not think it was a little price at all. No, it was a very great price. The Mukama had to sit in the *walifu* (alphabet) class with all the little children, and I, I had to give up my beautiful Nubian trousers (which were Muhammadan). Yes, it was a very great price." Preaching once on the nearness of Jesus, he said, "Yes, I know what it is to feel Jesus near. When I was in the chain gang, Jesus had hold of my hand."

'Apolo was no linguist. He lived out of his native country of Buganda for so many years, but he never lost his Luganda accent. But his preaching was most popular. Wherever he went, people crowded to hear him. When he came to the hospital the different ward services had to be given up so that all who could possibly hear him could be gathered into one ward, I think it must have been his extremely practical way. He talked with a great fund of very practical simple illustrations.'

Tailpiece

Some further memories of Apolo by Dr A. T. Schofield are included here to complete this portrait.

'From 1923 until his death, I had the privilege of knowing Apolo intimately, and of travelling with him. For weeks at a time we travelled together, walking the daily fifteen miles or so. Four of these journeys were into the deep parts of the Congo forest which he knew so well, and where he was so beloved. While he was Rural Dean of Toro I saw him almost daily.

'My greatest memory of Apolo is that everyone, no matter of what colour, creed or race, seemed to feel better and happier in his presence. No one could ignore him, however quietly he came in, and no one seemed able to frown or to be unkind in his presence. I cannot remember anyone else who so radiated joy and love. Children came running out, laughing and jumping about with joy when he came into a village. However unheralded, it soon got round that Apolo had come, and soon there was a crowd of young people following him wherever he went. It was "personality" in the modern sense, but through no sense of any conspicuous behaviour or imposing appearance—he was certainly not good looking, and was only a very slight figure—but just a glow that seemed to warm everyone.

'I remember a good example of this when I left him in my car while I made a call in a big new shop in the capital. I went to see the manager, a Jew. Almost as soon as I began to speak to the manager I noticed his attention was not on what I was saying (and it was quite important), so I repeated it rather sharply, when he said, "I am sorry, but do you know who is that wonderful old Uncle Sam standing in the doorway?" It was Apolo of course, who had got out of the car. Although there was quite a crowd, he was unknown, as far as I could see, to anyone but myself.

'Walking through the day's march in the forest, Apolo would call to one or other of the young teachers or young girls to walk with him for a little while, just as one could imagine Jesus did with his disciples, and every time, of course, it was obvious by the beaming face of the one who was honoured how very much they loved him for this special sign of his favour.

'Though Apolo was the very embodiment of warm and loving sympathy, he was very far from being a flabby, spineless individual. He would denounce sin in no uncertain voice, but he was very gentle with the repentant sinner. Yet he was very definite on the need for repentance, and his scorn was quite roused and fierce when he heard young men boasting and prideful, and even more so when he detected any racial feeling. In fact, on his last visit to Buganda, he gave up any thought of the rest he badly needed and went about preaching *Okutabaganyawamu* (be reconciled to each other) for he had quickly sensed the beginning of an anti-European feeling among young educated Baganda.

'I shall never forget his long and quite fierce address on this subject to my weekly Bible class, which usually consisted of twenty to thirty young educated men and chiefs. As he had been announced as the speaker, some 120 turned up and we had to move to a larger hall, so we were late in starting. Apolo was like an Old Testament prophet, in his intense fervour, and we finished long after sunset and in darkness.

'The main part of his talk was on reconciliation—*okutabaganyawamu* was the word he kept using (II Cor. 5.18–20)—reconciliation of the unbeliever, the wanderer, the sinner, and, most of all, our-ourselves, the Christians, with God, but also among ourselves—black and white. Again and again he kept returning with quite fierce denunciation of those Baganda—he kept saying, his "own people"—who criticized the whites. I shall never forget one dramatic symbol he used; the black and white Christians were like the legs of a table. If you took a leg away the top and the other legs fell and were useless.

'And then he started a really heavy personal attack on those who behaved like this. At last he broke off and after a silence he shouted a question; "What are you to do when you have these thoughts and say these things?" A long silence, a bit uncomfortable, and then, "No. I want *you* to *tell* me". Someone plucked up courage in the silence to say, "Stop thinking those thoughts". The old saint shouted, quite fiercely, "No! That is not enough!" Another uncomfortable silence, then he held up his hand and so very gently said, "No one will ever be able to know the love of God and teach it to anyone—to the heathen, to the sinner—until he is himself reconciled with God and everyone else. And when you have these thoughts there is only one thing to do. Enter into your inner room and pray, *pray*, PRAY—pray all night long and don't leave off until God has shown you your true self, what you are and what are your faults, and the Holy Spirit has shown you what is this 'ministry of reconciliation' that St Paul writes about". And then, in the stillness, he said, "I, Apolo, take these words of St Paul into my mouth". He read out verse 20, and then he repeated part of it as his own: "God beseeches you by me, Apolo. I pray you in Christ's stead, be ye reconciled". Then he had us all on our knees in prayer, and in that wonderful stillness he prayed for us all, white and black, to be united in God's service and for each other.

'Perhaps this also brings out Apolo's great courage, for, alone in

165

that audience, I knew as a doctor that Apolo very badly needed a complete rest. As a doctor, too, I had seen the scars and deformities on his body which he kept hidden, but which were the evidence of his terrible early experience at Mboga.

'An example of Apolo's humour was when I asked him once what were the great hindrances to the work of spreading the Gospel in the great Congo forest where he then worked. He answered at once: "Ticks, and the big animals—elephant and buffaloes." Of course, the so-called big game—buffalo, elephant, lion, etc., were a danger to all that travelled from village to village, but to put these against, and second to, the tiny ticks was amusing, but yet was a touch of his genius, for the ticks carried tick fever (or relapsing fever) for which there was then no easy cure, and Apolo's teachers who tried to penetrate through the forest succumbed one after another to this condition. In fact, Apolo said that if I could help him in finding a good treatment for tick fever which could be given to his teachers, I would have done the greatest of all services. This led to my discovery in 1927 of the treatment of this disease by Stovarsol, which was published in the medical press the same year.

'Another abiding memory of Apolo is of his unselfishness and his constant thought and planning for others. I have instanced his planting of the gum trees for the future church or school. I remember another time when I was preparing to return to England for furlough. I asked Apolo what I could suggest to our friends in England that they could send him. He spoke of books, money for schools, and so on. "Yes," I said, "we had all those things written down, but what could we ask them to send for him, himself?" Again he spoke of his teachers needing things like chairs and lamps so that they could read at night. Yes, we could get those, but what about something really for himself alone. Again the same thought, but this time footballs and so on for the boys, or other things for the girls. But I wanted to know of something specially for him and no one else.

'At last he said, "Well, he would really like a mackintosh coat and a waterproof bedroll, and perhaps a small tent." You see, it was always damp in the forest, and his old bones had begun to ache when he had to sleep on the ground on wet mats. And so it was himself last of all! Yet there was one little weakness that showed how human he was. He had quite a vanity in clothes. He had to have gold-framed reading glasses, not steel, even though the steel-framed perhaps were a little better. Clean and good clothes were definitely his need, and he had the very greatest pleasure when the boys at Eton, on my suggestion, sent him a new cassock, surplice and a canon's scarf when he was made a canon of the Church.

'Finally, some memories which may give some reasons why Apolo was—well, Apolo. One night when we were deep in the forest, I happened to wake up in my tent at about 2 a.m. I saw the light burning in Apolo's hut. I wondered if perhaps the old man was ill. However, all seemed perfectly quiet, so I went to sleep again. In the morning, as usual, a young teacher came to greet me and to enquire from Apolo if I had slept well. I asked this young man if Apolo had been unwell, and told him how I had seen the light burning in his hut. The young man answered, "If you wake up every night at that time, you will see the same light burning. You see, everyone wants to see Apolo all day and he never refuses anyone. He has no time to himself during the day. So then 'when the ashes on the hearth grow cold' [a way of telling the time—it would be about 2 a.m.] he wakes up and spends an hour reading and praying."

'Another episode was when the Uganda Jubilee celebrations took place in 1927. I had brought Apolo down to the capital for these, and we went together to different events. One of the events was a pageant of the first young martyrs in 1885. On one side of me was sitting Apolo, and on the other Ham Mukasa, while near us was another, Mika Sematimba, who, with Ham Mukasa, was one of those very same young men, pages of the King, who had been condemned to be burnt to death because they refused to renounce their Christian faith. Humanly speaking, both Ham and Mika were only alive today by a miracle, while Apolo's own story too is linked with that very first martyrdom. These men, therefore, were witnessing the acting of scenes in their own lives, and it was because of those very scenes long ago that they each had that wonderful

reality and certainty of Christian experience and faith to which
their lives witnessed—what it really meant to be a Christian. I
could see then, in a very dim way, the meaning to these men of that
text I had often heard Apolo preach upon, "To me, to live is
Christ".'

TWO SONGS ABOUT APOLO

The Song of the Forest People

	Chorus
Formerly I used to commit	*Now I am full of great joy*
The sins of Satan,	*Because of the word of Jesus,*
But Jesus the Saviour	*He is the King of Love,*
Came and took them from me.	*He is the unfailing friend.*
This Jesus came to earth	*(Repeat)*
To take away sins	
From people who believe	
And to give them life.	
Jesus the Lord was killed	*(Repeat)*
To redeem people,	
All of us bad people,	
To take away our sins.	
Now Jesus is with	*(Repeat)*
God our Father,	
He is the mediator	
Between God and man.	
He will come back on earth	*Now let us all leap,*
To take you where He is,	*For the message of Apolo,*
All of us who love Him	*Apolo Kivebulaya,*
With all our hearts.	*A valiant fighter.*

Let us all think   *(Repeat)*
About him who warned us,
Apolo Kivebulaya,
Who loved the forest.

Who befriended the Abambuti?   *My spirit rejoices*
Who loved them greatly?   *When I think of Apolo,*
It is Apolo Kivebulaya,   *Apolo Kivebulaya,*
A great lover.   *A valiant fighter.*

Kivebulaya is with   *(Repeat)*
God the Son.
He will never be forgotten by the
    Abambuti
Nor by any of us.

Apolo stressed it to us   *We all get new strength*
Never to leave Jesus.   *When we sing about Apolo,*
Thus we must always remember *The hero of God,*
All that is stressed to us.   *For him let us conquerors be.*
                              Amen.

A Song about Apolo

Apolo Apolo Kivebulaya,
He it was who became the friend of the Pygmies.
Where he preached the Gospel of Christ,
When he went on journeys for Christ.

Apolo Apolo Kivebulaya,
He who befriended the Pygmies
And preached to them the Gospel of Christ.

Apolo Apolo Kivebulaya,
A truly brave man,
Who also spent himself for Christ,
And they afflicted him for Christ,
And they beat him with rods for Christ.

Apolo Apolo Kivebulaya,
His spirit was satisfied
When he converted the Pygmies to Christ,
And they were saved for Christ,
When he died he rejoiced for Christ's sake.

NOTES

[1] Taken by Dr A. T. Schofield, C.M.S. missionary doctor in Toro.

[2] 'But the harvest of the spirit is love, joy, peace, patience, kindness, goodness, fidelity, gentleness and self-control.' *The New English Bible*.

[3] Two incidents only are recorded. In his diary Apolo mentions pushing an insolent man out of his house in anger. It is also mentioned that he once kicked a lazy porter who would not get up and carry his load.

[4] The *amagasani* or burial shrines of the *Bito* kings of Bunyoro and Toro are places of pagan religious significance. The keeper of a king's burial shrine would originally be one of his wives, her place being inherited by her daughter or another female relative. I have not been able to trace the whereabouts of this shrine, but it is most probably in the Myeri area of Mwenge, where the first Mukama of Toro set himself up as an independent ruler. See K. Ingham, 'The Amagasani of the Abakama of Bunyoro', *Uganda Journal*, vol. 17 (1953), pp. 138–45.

[5] Bishop Balaya.

[6] Rev. Yusufu Limenya.

[7] Rev. Tomasi Ndahura.

[8] Peradarsi Kahwa.

[9] Rev. W. S. R. Russell.

[10] Nasani Kabarole.

[11] Ruben Kakonge.

[12] Rev. Asa Byara.

[13] Yoweri Rwakaikara.

APPENDIX A

Notes on Apolo's diaries

At some time Apolo had obviously been urged by the European missionaries to write down the experiences of his ministry, especially the early dramatic events at Mboga. The first book into which he wrote these experiences is an exercise book with a shabby shiny black cover. 'This book is the first I have written about my work for our Lord. I, Apolo Kivebulaya.' There are two sets of entries for the years 1894–9 at either end of the book. These appear to have been copied by someone else, as the handwriting is not Apolo's. One version is briefer than the other, but they are essentially the same. The rest of the book is a muddle of entries, mostly in Apolo's handwriting, up to the year 1921; seldom are the entries in consecutive order, which may mean that they were copied in at some later date from more complete annual diaries. On the other hand, the entries for many of the years are fairly full and detailed; he may actually have used this book as a diary, it is old and tattered and well thumbed; also various letters he had received were pasted in it.

There is also a translation in my possession of what appears to have been a small diary (now lost) containing yet another account, brief, but similar to the others, of the years 1891–9. There are entries for the years 1903–5, and a brief history of the Mukama Daudi Kasagama of Toro.

In another 'black book' (now in Namirembe Cathedral) begun in 1922, Apolo gives a short account of his early life from infancy to the time of his baptism, and yet another account of the Mboga persecution—leaving out much of the original part of the story. Then follow copies of letters Apolo had received from time to time and extracts from diaries for 1918–19, 1922–9. For some years there are no entries—perhaps the original diaries were lost; also pages are missing here and there.

For 1931 we have a complete day-to-day diary which gives us

some useful insight into his daily activities. Last of all there is a small pocket diary for 1933 (in the C.M.S. Archives) with daily entries up to a month before his death. This also contains a prayer written on the last page, perhaps when he first received the diary. (*See* Apolo's prayer, p. 137.)

All Apolo's diaries were written in Luganda and have been translated into English by Mrs Lucy Ridsdale and Miss Alice Sebigaju. Those in my possession will be placed in the Makerere College Archives.

APPENDIX B

A brief assessment of the existing literature on Apolo

Archdeacon A. B. Lloyd—a biographical note

Archdeacon Lloyd has been the main authority for the existing literature on Apolo. I therefore include the following biographical note.

A. B. Lloyd arrived in Uganda as a lay missionary in 1895. He was stationed in Toro during the years 1896–8. He visited Mboga twice during those years, when he went over in August 1896 with A. B. Fisher and again in January 1897. He was later stationed in Bunyoro. In November 1909 he was ordained to the priesthood at Namirembe. He was sent again to Toro in 1911, where he served as Rural Dean, and finally as Archdeacon of Western Uganda until April 1925, when he retired. In 1928 he visited Uganda, which included a visit to his old friend Apolo at Mboga. After Apolo's death in 1933 he accepted one year's (1934) service at Mboga to help establish a European missionary there. He died on 13 December 1946, aged 75.

Three books on Apolo by A. B. Lloyd

Apolo of the Pygmy Forest (C.M.S. 1923).

More about Apolo (C.M.S. 1928)

Apolo the Pathfinder—who Follows? (C.M.S. 1934).

These little books were written as missionary propaganda. Archdeacon Lloyd was a devoted and much-loved missionary, but his uncritical writings leave much to be desired. There is no regard for historical accuracy and there are discrepancies between his stories of the persecution suffered by Apolo and Apolo's own account as related in this book. As will be seen in Chapter IV of *Apolo of the Pygmy*

Forest, Lloyd relates four dramatic stories of the persecution Apolo suffered at Mboga in 1898.

(1) The Mukama of Mboga sends his men to burn Apolo alive in his hut at night; while doing this they hear the voice of God telling them to desist, as Apolo is His servant. They then rescue the praying Apolo from the enveloping flames.

(2) Later the Mukama sends his men to bind Apolo, who disarms his captors by preaching to them. They release him and face the fury of their master.

(3) As Apolo still refuses to leave the country, he is brought before the Mukama and severely beaten with a hippohide whip, but undaunted Apolo recovers and continues his work.

(4) Again he is dragged before the Mukama and beaten to within an inch of his life, his unconscious body being flung into the long grass for the wild beasts to devour. However, a faithful convert, whom Apolo has defended against a cruel husband finds his body, in which there is still a spark of life, and she secretly nurses him back to health, whereupon the triumphant Apolo returns, as from the dead, to beat the church drum to call the faithful. The terrified Mukama throws himself upon his knees to beg forgiveness, declaring, with tears coursing down his cheeks, that from henceforth he is God's man and will serve Him to the end. These accounts are greatly at variance with those of Apolo's diary and surviving witnesses.

In Chapter V of *Apolo of the Pygmy Forest* Lloyd perhaps confuses the Balega rising of 1911, when Mboga remained untouched, with the Manyuema raids of 1897, when Mboga was looted and burned.

In *Apolo the Pathfinder—who Follows?* Chapter II, the story of the conversion of the first Balega village in 1906 could not have happened thus, as Apolo was in Toro from 1899 to 1915, and there is no evidence that he visited Mboga during 1906. The story of the Mulega spearman falling before Apolo was told by Yoweri Rwakaikara and probably happened on a return journey from Geti in 1921.

A. B. Lloyd's assessment of Apolo's character—see *Apolo of the Pygmy Forest* (New and Enlarged Edition 1936), pp. 44–46—is entirely in accordance with the accounts of others. Also of value in these little books are the foreword and preface by Bishop J. J. Willis of Uganda in *Apolo of the Pygmy Forest* (first edition) and *Apolo the Pathfinder—who Follows?* respectively. Also a description of Apolo's passing by the Rev. W. S. R. Russell in the latter volume.

Did Apolo know about these books by A. B. Lloyd? It might be noted here that Apolo could not read English and there is no record of his having received a copy of either of the first two books.

In a letter to Apolo written from London, dated 27 May 1924, Lloyd says: 'Many Christians are reading that book which *we wrote* . . .' This I presume refers to the book *Apolo of the Pygmy Forest*. Lloyd may have been the one who urged Apolo to write his experiences, but one wonders very much whether Apolo ever knew of the largely fictional version Lloyd gave of his experiences! I am inclined to think not. Although Bishop Willis and the missionaries in Uganda all believed Lloyd's stories, not one of the people I asked about the persecution stories of Apolo, either in Toro or Mboga, had ever heard Lloyd's version. When asked about the four dramatic stories told by Lloyd, Yoweri Rwakaikara said they were never told of them by Apolo, but he often recounted to them the events of the 'spear tragedy'. They all retailed these events more or less as Apolo himself recorded them in the first 'black book', including Tomasi Ndahura, who strangely enough, wrote an article entitled 'Make Him to be Numbered with Thy Saints' for the magazine *Ebifa* (no date given, but I suspect it was late in 1933 or early in 1934) retailing almost verbatim the Lloyd stories. A possible explanation is that the Rev. A. J. Binaisa from Buganda had temporarily come to Mboga to take over Apolo's work on 17 June 1933 (see a letter from Rev. A. J. Binaisa to *Ebifa*, 2 September 1933), no doubt bringing with him the Lloyd version of the persecution stories, it was probably he who persuaded Tomasi to write this article.

Books and publications based on A. B. Lloyd's authority

W. J. Roome, *Apolo, The Apostle to the Pygmies*, Marshall, Morgan and Scott Ltd. (1934).

A small book probably written for children, repeating almost verbatim all Lloyd's stories, with the addition of more information about the little people of Pygmyland.

Mr Roome was for some years Secretary for East Africa of the British and Foreign Bible Society. He travelled widely in East Africa and visited Mboga with Lloyd in 1928. He died in 1937.

Pat Yates, *Apolo in Pygmyland*, Eagle Books No. 29, Highway Press (1940).

Margaret Sinker, *Into the Great Forest*, Highway Press (1950).

Both these works of fiction are based entirely on Lloyd's stories.

M. L. Braby, *Four Lessons on Apolo*, C.M.S.

A small pamphlet for Bible-class study based on Lloyd's books.

G. R. Katongole, *Apolo Kivebulaya owe Mbooga*, Uganda Bookshop Press (1952).

A small book written in Luganda. It is based partly on what was locally known about Apolo, but Lloyd is obviously the authority for the section on Mboga.

More Accurate Accounts of the Persecutions of Apolo at Mboga

Alfred R. Tucker, Bishop of Uganda 1890–1911, wrote the first account of how Christianity came to Mboga, when describing a visit he made to Toro and Mboga in 1898. Alfred R. Tucker, *Toro Visits to Ruwenzori*, C.M.S. (1899). pp. 48–49. Alfred R. Tucker, *Eighteen Years in Uganda and East Africa*, Edward Arnold (1908), vol. ii, pp. 139–42. Other accounts are also to be found in—

T. B. Johnson, *Tramps round the Mountains of the Moon*, T. Fisher Unwin (1912), pp. 149–50.

T. R. Buckley, 'Some Experiences in Uganda', *Uganda Church Review* (March 1933), pp. 31–32.

W. E. Geil, *A Yankee in Pygmyland*, Hodder and Stoughton (1905), p. 158.

Bishop Aberi Balya has written an account of the persecution stories, which are also fully told by the following—Yakobo Tabinderana, Ibrahimu Katalibara, Nasani Kabarole.

APPENDIX C

A list of people who have known Apolo and have contributed to this biography

In Toro

Bishop Aberi Balya is a Mutoro. He was ordained in 1920 and was assistant Bishop of the Uganda Diocese from 1947 to 1960. He knew Apolo from 1895. 'He prepared me for confirmation in 1902 and for the catechist's first certificate in 1904.' They were life-long friends and he has written a short memoir on Apolo.

T. B. Bazarrabusa, M.B.E., is a Mukonjo from the Ruwenzori Mountains. Formerly Minister for Education in the Toro Government. He is now Uganda's High Commissioner in Britain.

Erisaniya Munubi is a Mutoro. As a lad of 10 years he came into Apolo's house in 1910, and stayed with him for about five years. After he left he went astray. He lived in Busoga for some time. He had a hymn book with him which he read sometimes, then he bought himself a Bible and returned to Kabarole, where he became a verger in the church. He is now retired.

Rev. A. Byara comes from the cattle people of Mwenge district in Toro. He was baptized by Apolo. He first trained as a school teacher and was later ordained to the ministry, and is now in charge of a large urban parish in Kampala.

Rev. Yosiya Kamuhigi is a Mutoro. He was born in 1880 and baptized in 1899. Kamuhigi was a Gombolola chief. He said it was Apolo who brought him to Christ and showed him that being a clergyman was more important than being a chief. He was ordained in 1909. The Mukama gave him the village of Bosaiga for his support. He is now retired.

Rev. Andereya Sere is a Mutoro from Butiti; he was baptized there in 1897. He knew Apolo when he was there in 1901–2. The Rev. A. L. Kitching writes of him in 1902, 'He has for a long time taken an active part in the teaching work at this station and has now determined, if God will, to consecrate himself definitely to the Lord's work and to become a candidate for the Ministry . . . I believe him to be a truly converted man.' Apolo married Andereya and Leya at Kabarole in 1900. He was ordained a priest in November 1909. He was given a portion of land by the Mukama, upon which he now lives in retirement.

Edward Winyi is a Mutoro born in 1901, the son of Chief Bartolomayo Rusongoza. He knew Apolo in 1907. Apolo always looked upon their home as 'his' because they had twins in the family (Apolo was a twin), the father of twins was also 'his father'.

Esiri Nyakabwa is a Mutoro. She is now a widow. She remembers Apolo from about 1901, when she was 13 years old. She became a church teacher, and all the teachers met in Apolo's house. The Mukama gave her two pieces of land for her support. He did this for all the teachers. She helped in the big classes at the church and also in the small school. She went visiting in the homes and villages with Miss Pike.

Rev. Ezekieri Binyomo is a Mutoro; he was born about 1888. The name Binyomo means an ant! He was given this name by his mother because an ant bit him on the ear when he was a baby, as he lay upon the floor of the hut. Ezekieri became a teacher and was sent to teach chief Bomera at his headquarters at Mbudu in the Balega country in 1910.

At Mboga

Yakobo Tebinderana is a Munyamboga. When Apolo first went to Mboga in December 1896 he was a lad of about 15 years old. He was sent by Tabaro to look after Apolo and serve him—the usual courtesy towards a visitor to the country with the Chief's approval—Yakobo was amongst the first group to be baptized by Rev. J. S. Callis in April 1897. He is still alive.

Ibrahimu Katalibara is a Munyamboga; he was also in the first group to be baptized at Mboga, and was confirmed in Toro in 1909. He later became a teacher and was in charge at Mboga for a short time after Apolo's death. He is still alive.

Nasani Kabarole is a Munyamboga; he was taught by Apolo when quite a boy. He then went to the forest to help Apolo and finally was left for a time to teach what he knew himself.

Rev. Tomasi Ndahura is a Munyamboga from Bulei; he attended classes taken by the teacher Ibrahimu in the church at Bulei. He first met Apolo in 1917 and was baptized by him in 1919. In 1921 he went to the forest as a teacher. Ordained in 1948, he was in charge of the Budingiri Pastorate for some years. He is now at Bukiringi among the Balega.

Rev. Yusufu Limenya is a Mukonjo from the forest. He was one of the teachers trained by Apolo, who was later ordained and put in charge of the Forest Pastorate at Kainama for many years. He is now working amonst the Baamba at Bubande.

Peradarsi Kahwa is a married woman living near the mission at Mboga. Her name Kahwa means the-child-that-is-the-one-to-follow-the-one that-follows-twins; the name can be used for either sex. She had worked for Apolo for just one year as his helper in the house. She came first to 'read' in the class at Mboga, and then went with a sick relative to the hospital at Toro. When Apolo came over there in 1927 as Rural Dean, she became a member of his household.

Yoweri Rwakaikara is a Munyamboga from Bulei. He is now one of the church teachers at Mboga. He was taken into Apolo's house while he was 'reading' for baptism; he was baptized in 1917. After his confirmation he was sent as a teacher to Buguje. He said that while he was stationed there he would go miles out of his way to avoid going through the Bulega country; they were still so wild in those days.

Rev. Fesito Byakisaka is a Munyamboga. His father was a sub-chief in the Mboga district. When his father died Apolo helped his widowed mother. Fesito was taught by Apolo and became a teacher in 1928, then he was sent to the forest to teach the Bahuku. He knew the cannibal, Bantumangia, whom Apolo baptized. 'He was a jolly fellow!' Fesito was ordained in 1950. In 1957 he was in charge of the Mboga Pastorate, including Budingiri and Kainama.

Yosia Kaburwa is a Munyamboga. At the age of 12 years he came to live in Apolo's house in 1920. Later he became a church teacher. Yoweri Rwakaikara and Tomasi Ndahura were lads in Apolo's house at that time also. They all helped with the housework and carried loads on safari. There were also some girls in the household and an old widow called Teresa. Apolo paid the 60s bride wealth for Yosia's marriage. Yosia was a teacher at Bwakadi in the forest for some time.

Dolosi Nyakaisiki is a Munyamboga. She was a young widow in Apolo's day; her husband had been a church teacher; her two children also died. She could read the Bible and so was sent as a teacher to Kainama, together with Basimasi Tagira. She first lived in the church care-taker's house, but later had one of her own. She taught the Bakonjo women and children at Kainama for five years. She came back to Mboga for refreshment and further training at intervals, also in times of famine in the forest, as violent storms often destroyed the *bitoke* and wild animals trampled or ate up the crops. (It was a church rule that every teacher must have a garden.) The refresher classes were held by Apolo and Yosia Kaburwa and consisted of Bible study, discussion of difficulties and problems. Dolosi never married again. She now lives near the Mission at Mboga.

Nduru is a Munyamboga. He came from the Roman Catholic Mission near Mboga. He is one of the oldest surviving people in these parts. He remembers Kabarega's warriors raiding over towards Mboga. He himself as a small child was captured and taken to Kabarega's court in Bunyoro, along with many others, who eventually returned, but he stayed on. He was in Bunyoro when H. M. Stanley's Emin Relief Expedition passed through Mboga (12 May 1889). He grew up there and then returned to Mboga, where he became one of the Mukama Tabaro's warriors. He remembers the Manyuema raids in 1897 and the Balega rising in 1911.

In Buganda

Ruben Kakonge is a Muganda, the son of Yakobo L. Musajalumbwa. He was educated at Budo school. He said: 'When the Principal of Budo asked for volunteers who could become "The Budo Adventurers" in the work of the dark forest of the Belgian Congo, I felt it right for me to volunteer and go and help that old man Canon Apolo Kivebulaya.' He built an 'Apolo Memorial' church near Nabutiti. He now lives at Mukono.

Lezoni Gitta Kibuka is a Muganda. Son of Zebidayo Kibuka, a relative of Canon Apolo Kivebulaya. He lives on the *Katinvuma* clan lands on Nabutiti hill about fourteen miles north of Kampala. Apolo's father and mother came to live on this land in their old age. They died and were buried there. Their graves are to be seen to this day on the top of the hill, marked by a border of stones. A man and his first (princi-pal) wife are buried side by side. Other wives are buried elsewhere. Gitta Kibuka is a landowner of considerable means. A tall courteous, man, his facial features bear a likeness to Apolo.

Europeans

Rev. W. S. R. Russell was a missionary in Uganda from 1910 to 1939. He first came to Toro in 1916 and was there until after Apolo died in 1933.

Miss Sarah Lyon was a nursing sister at Toro Mission hospital in 1933.

Dr A. T. Schofield was a missionary doctor in Toro for many years. Wrote a short memoir of Apolo.

Mrs G. E. Schofield, wife of Dr Schofield. Also wrote a short memoir of Apolo.

Miss E. M. E. Baring-Gould, already noted in Chapter 11. After a life-long association with C.M.S., died in London on 1 July 1961, aged 90.

Bishop Kitching. A pioneer missionary. He took over the Butiti mission station from Apolo in 1902 for some years. Later he was Archdeacon of Uganda and in 1926 was consecrated the first bishop of the new Diocese of the Upper Nile. He died 25 October 1960.

Mrs Ruth B. Fisher. Wife of the pioneer missionary to Toro, the Rev. A. B. Fisher. As Miss Ruth Hurditch she came to Toro in 1900. Author of *On the Borders of Pygmyland* and *Twilight Tales of the Black Baganda*. Died 15 November 1959.

GLOSSARY

Note:—*ganda* is the root from which are formed *Buganda*, the country; *Baganda*, the people; *Muganda*, a single person; *Luganda*, the language. *Uganda* is the Kiswahili form applied by the first explorers, and now embraces the present-day Uganda Protectorate. Similarly *nyoro* is the root from which are formed *Bunyoro*, the country; *Banyoro*, the people; *Munyoro*, a single person; *Lunyoro*, the language.

Luganda words

bainda, young men of Kabaka Mwanga's bodyguard.
balubale (sing. *lubale*), hero-gods.
Banubi, Nubians.
Basese, people of the Sese Islands.
Bavuma, people of Buvuma Island near the exit of the Nile.
Bazungu, Europeans.
Bulozi, Governor or administrator.
Futabangi, 'hemp-smokers', a pagan rebel movement.
Gombolola, division of a county.
Kabaka, title of the hereditary ruler of Buganda.
Katikiro, title of the Chief Minister.
Kisalosalo, Major-domo of the Kabaka's court.
Lubiri, the Kabaka's enclosure.
mateka, first Luganda reading book printed by Mackay in 1880.
mizimu (sing. *muzimu*), human spirits.
muganga, a witch-doctor who deals in antidotes and protection against spells.
Mukwenda, title of the county chief of Singo.
Mulongo, the twin.
Muwanika, chief storekeeper of the Kabaka's court.
Namasole, Queen Mother.
Pokino, title of the county chief of Buddu.
saza, district or county.
Sekibobo, title of the county chief of Kyagwe.
walifu, alphabet.

Lunyoro words

bitoke, boiled plantains, the staple diet of Buganda and the agricultural people of Toro and Bunyoro.

empako, praise name.

kikale, Mukama's enclosure.

Mukama, hereditary ruler of Bunyoro, Toro, and Mboga.

mufumu, sorcerer.

nyakatagara, diviner.

Nyina Mukama, Queen Mother.

Rukunato, council of chiefs.

Kiswahili words

frasila, a measure of weight, about 36 lb.

joho, long loose-sleeved Arab coat.

jura of *amerikani*, 30-yard bolt of American calico.

kanzu, long white robe introduced by the Arabs.

Waganda, Baganda.

Ulaya, England.

INDEX OF PERSONAL NAMES

INDEX OF SUBJECTS